GHOST
TOWNS *Alive*

GHOST TOWNS *Alive*

TRIPS TO NEW MEXICO'S PAST

LINDA G. HARRIS

PHOTOGRAPHS BY PAMELA PORTER

University of New Mexico Press   ❊   Albuquerque

ISBN-13: 978-0-8263-2908-0
ISBN-10: 0-82-63-2908-x

Library of Congress Cataloging-in-Publication Data
Harris, Linda G.
   Ghost towns alive! : trips to New Mexico's past /
Linda G. Harris ; photographs by Pamela Porter.— 1st ed.
      p. cm.
Includes bibliographical references and index.
   ISBN 0-8263-2907-1 (cloth : alk. paper) —
ISBN 0-8263-2908-x (pbk. : alk. paper)
   1. Ghost towns—New Mexico—Guidebooks.
2. New Mexico—History, Local.   3. Automobile
travel—New Mexico—Guidebooks.   4. New Mexico—
Guidebooks.   I. Title.
F797 .G47 2003
917.8904'54—dc21

                                    2003009194

Design: Melissa Tandysh

For Jim,
and for Scott

Contents

Preface

My reasons for exploring New Mexico's ghost towns grew out of practical curiosity. A few years ago, while researching *Houses in Time*, a book about New Mexico homes, I went in search of a house in a true ghost town. I discovered instead that most of New Mexico's ghost towns are still alive. A few, in fact, are downright lively.

In this practical mode, I discarded *Webster's* definition of a ghost town as "permanently abandoned" and instead wrote my own. A ghost town, in my way of thinking, is a town brought to life for a specific reason—say, mining, or the railroad, or ranching. The town prospers for a time, then some event, or turning point, causes it to decline. But not necessarily to die. Out of curiosity, I looked for reasons that allowed some towns to survive and others to reinvent themselves altogether.

The ghost towns in this book are accessible and visually interesting. Once or twice, a town doesn't have much to see, but it does have the saving grace of its history or its beauty. I visited each town at least once from August 2001 to July 2002. While I benefited from half a dozen ghost town books dating back fifty years, the bulk of my information comes from interviews, journal articles, specialized histories, local histories, and archeological reports.

Although I give directions to each town and make note of their museums, my aim is not to be a tour guide. For that, readers will have to depend on their own curiosity and common sense. But do take plenty of water, a shovel, and lunch. And do take a map—I used the *New Mexico Road and Recreation Atlas* and the more detailed *The Roads of New Mexico*. The internet is a great tool for ghost towning. Many of the museums, some of the towns, and all of the counties have web sites.

My goal as a writer is to take readers along without having them leave home. But my hope is that the book will spur them to get up and go themselves. Pamela Porter's goal as photographer is to underscore a sense of place while adding visual interest.

❧

What began as an exercise in curiosity turned out to be a personal adventure. My earliest travels came during a time of national anguish. As I crossed New Mexico's northern mesas I found the vast open spaces a comfort, an old mining town reassuring. This might have been true of any September. What I found in these towns were not ghosts, but the essence of lives spent making a living and in some cases making history. There is a reverence to these towns stilled in time. That was my most important, and my most surprising, discovery.

In my ghost town travels, most of my discoveries were encouraging. For starters, the roads are better. In the ghost towns themselves, churches are being restored and draw generations back for reunions. Schools make good community centers, spacious libraries, and roomy homes. Historic preservation has many faces—from the park ranger who gives walking tours, to the couple who run the family museum, to the artisans who have brought a whole town back to life. Museums are everywhere. Local historians, bless them, are writing the histories of these lost places.

Other discoveries, however, are really old problems. Treasure hunters have picked many a town clean and vandals have destroyed others. I've found that two places are most vulnerable to destruction: those where no one is in sight and those too close to the road. The way to keep a ghost town alive is for someone to live there, or at least keep a watchful eye on it. My biggest gripe, though, is with cows. They push against fragile adobes to scratch an itch. They snack on cemetery grass and trample over graves. They leave evidence everywhere. The solution is to fence the cemeteries, and in some cases entire towns, on the open range.

❧

While the travel brought me both adventure and renewal, it was not a solo trip. I had at my side a legion of companions who gave me the generous loan of their advice, expertise, and encouragement. I am grateful to them all.

First mention should go to those who staff the museums and parks at New Mexico's ghost towns. Some are individuals whose collections reflect a rich family heritage, some are newcomers who have taken up the cause of history, while others are professionals dedicated to preserving historical sites. Appreciation goes to Sara and L.Y. Jackson at Ancho's House of Old Things; David Johnson at the Carson National Forest; Don and Donna Edmund at the Pioneer Store Museum at Chloride; Patrick Rand at the Sacramento Mountains Historical Museum at Cloudcroft; Armando Martinez and Brian

Houltin at the Pancho Villa State Park at Columbus; Bill Ward at the Columbus Historical Museum; Fred Kilian at the Fort Stanton Museum; the staff at the Fort Union National Monument; Shelby Caddell at the Lake Valley Schoolhouse Museum; Frances Schafer and her son Bob Schaefer at the Pinos Altos Museum; Jason Schubert at the Philmont Museum at Rayado; Janaloo Hill and her husband, Manny Hough, at Shakespeare; Susan Berry and Jim Carlson at the Silver City Museum; Linda and Larry Link at Steins; Sarah Wood at the Sugarite Canyon State Park; and Robert W. Leslie at the White Oaks Museum.

Thanks to the many who welcomed us into their towns, gave us information, and on occasion fed us: Restie and Annie Sandoval at Cabezon; Don Houser at Chance City; Maryann Champion at Cimarron; Benolyn McKibbin and Frank DuBois at Claunch; Richard Dean at Columbus; Thelma Winnie at Cuchillo; Lucy Kalec Tomchak at Dawson; Eloy Montoya at La Bajada; Benito C' de Baca at Loma Parda; Clair Cundiff, Linda Dunhill, and Dakota Herkenhoff at Madrid; John McClendon, the friendly face at Mogollon; Bill Ward at Orogrande; David Kirkpatrick and Melhi Duran, Margaret Laumbach and her son, Karl Laumbach, Charles Chambers and Marilyn Decker, all for information on the Ring Place; Frank Franco at Trementina; and Rudy Tenero and Andrew Lavato at San Luis.

Many authors and researchers helped build the foundation for this book. Many are listed in the Selected Readings, but a few warrant special mention: Donald Couchman for his meticulous research on Cookes Peak, Nasario García for his books on the Rio Puerco towns, Philip Varney for his guide *New Mexico's Best Ghost Towns*, Ralph Looney for *Haunted Highways*, James E. and Barbara Sherman for *Ghost Towns and Mining Camps of New Mexico*, and Robert Julyan for *The Place Names of New Mexico*.

My appreciation goes to the libraries who loaned me books and the librarians who helped me with the facts: Don Wiltshire at the Magdalena Public Library; the staffs of the Rio Grande Historical Collections and of Special Collections at the New Mexico State University Library; Arthur Olivas at the Palace of the Governors, Museum of New Mexico; plus the reference librarians at the New Mexico State Library and Records Center.

Thanks to Russell Bamert and Debra Weaver for loaning me their collection of ghost town books, Pat Beckett for help in finding out-of-print books, and Bob Anderson for Rio Puerco sources. Appreciation also goes to my friends the Friday writers and to Leslie Blair for her editorial advice.

I could not have asked for a more supportive family. My love and thanks go to my mother, Mary Thompson, for being my biblical source; to my daughter, Christine Strickland, and her family for allowing me to use their home as my travel headquarters; to my grandson, Austin Harris, for being my note-taking assistant; and especially to my husband, Jim Harris, for driving his 1992 Ford truck on the back roads and for his critical eye as my first line editor.

Photographer Pamela Porter gives a special thank-you to Scott Vance, who offered encouragement and assistance in every aspect of the photography within these pages. The map-reading skills and support of part-time traveling companion Alison Bamert are also appreciated.

And finally, thanks to the staff of the University of New Mexico Press for making it all work.

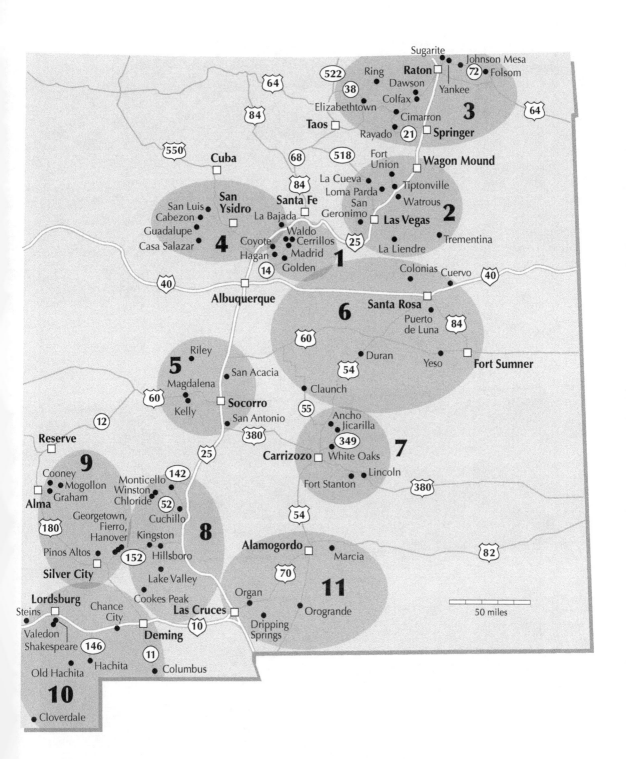

Sugarite

64

522

38

Ring   Raton
Dawson
Johnson Mesa
72 Folsom
Yankee

Colfax

Elizabethtown   Cimarron

84

Taos   Rayado   21   Springer   3   64

68   518   Fort
Union   Wagon Mound

550   Cuba

84   La Cueva   Tiptonville
Loma Parda   Watrous

San   Ysidro   Santa Fe   San
Geronimo   2

San Luis   La Bajada   Las Vegas
Cabezon   Waldo   Cerrillos
Guadalupe   4   Coyote   Madrid   25   La Liendre   Trementina
Casa Salazar   Hagan   Golden   1

14   Colonias   Cuervo   40
40   Albuquerque   6   Santa Rosa
Puerto
de Luna   84

60   Duran
Riley   Yeso   Fort Sumner
5   San Acacia   54
Magdalena   Claunch
60   Socorro   55
12   Kelly   San Antonio   Ancho
Jicarilla   7
Reserve   380   349
25   Carrizozo   White Oaks
Cooney   142   Fort Stanton   Lincoln
Mogollon   Monticello   52   380
9   Graham   Winston   Chloride   54
Alma   Cuchillo   Alamogordo
Georgetown,   Marcia   82
Fierro,   Kingston   8
Hanover   152   Hillsboro   70
Pinos Altos   11
Silver City   Lake Valley   Organ   Orogrande
Lordsburg   Chance   Cookes Peak   Las Cruces
Steins   City   10   Dripping
Valedon   Springs
Shakespeare   146   Deming   50 miles
Old Hachita   11
Hachita   Columbus
10
Cloverdale

xiii

· 1 ·

Turquoise Trail:
From Turquoise to Tourists

Cerrillos · Waldo · Madrid · Golden · Hagan · Coyote

In 1540 Francisco Vásquez de Coronado led an expedition of 336 Spaniards, 100 Indians, and 559 horses into New Mexico, looking for gold. The young nobleman, led on by fanciful reports of the Seven Cities of Gold, chased the hoax all the way to Kansas before giving up. The thinking was that since Mexico's northern provinces were producing great mineral wealth, so would *Nuevo México*. Undaunted by Coronado's failure, Spain then awarded the right to colonize New Mexico to Juan de Oñate, whose father owned the largest silver mine in Mexico. Oñate also used his father's fortune to finance his 1598 expedition. Not only did Oñate fail to repeat his father's success, he ended his term as governor broke and in exile.

New Mexico did hold silver and gold and many, many other minerals, but four centuries ago no one knew where. Until the Spanish arrived, mining in New Mexico primarily had been a quarry operation with natives prospecting riverbeds and canyons for pottery clay or mining hillsides for building stones. Natives did trade in turquoise, which they prized for both its ornamental and ceremonial value. Turquoise beads found at the Chaco Canyon pueblos probably came from mines near Cerrillos, indicating that the mines date back at least a thousand years. Coal ash found in even older ruins also shows that coal was mined in New Mexico as long as 12,000 years ago.

In 1828 New Mexico finally yielded a cache of gold in the Ortiz Mountains between Golden and Madrid, making it the oldest gold-mining district in the United States. However, isolation and Indian troubles stalled mining development until the 1860s. By then the rush for gold in California and Colorado had spilled into New Mexico.

The United States at first took a hands-off approach to mining in its newly acquired territories. But with the Mining Law of 1866 the government allowed free access to public lands and guaranteed a prospector the rights to

In various states of disrepair and renovation, these old miners' cottages line NM Highway 14, which bisects the former company town of Madrid, where coal mines flourished in spurts until after World War II.

his discovery. He had only to prove he had discovered a mineral on the claim and have it verified by an assay. To retain his claim, the miner had to make $100 worth of improvements a year on his mine, a total that could include his pay of $4 a day. The law applied to both placer mining, which involved minerals washed down from a lode into stream and gravel beds, and lode mining, which involved minerals concentrated in a vein between layers of bedrock. The placer method was both easier and more profitable in the early days of gold mining in New Mexico. However, because placer mining required large amounts of water to separate out the gold—water that was nearly as scarce as the gold itself—its profitability also proved fleeting.

The mining towns of this era saw boom and bust in the best ghost town tradition. Today Madrid, Cerrillos, and Golden are once again alive while Waldo, Hagan, and Coyote barely exist outside the imagination.

Cerrillos

Cerrillos is located on the scenic Turquoise Trail 24 miles south of Santa Fe and 3 miles north of Madrid on NM 14.

"The earth is filled with gold, silver, and turquoise," the Spanish explorer Antonio de Espejo wrote of his visit to New Mexico in 1583. His bold claim may also have applied to the "little hills" from which Cerrillos gets its name. At least a thousand years ago in these hills Pueblo Indians chipped pieces of blue-green rock they called *chalchihuitl*, the Aztec word for turquoise.

When the Spaniards came, however, their interests lay in the veins of silver inside Chalchihuitl Mountain. They used slave labor from the nearby Tano Pueblo to excavate silver from deep inside the Mina de la Tierra. In an oft-repeated account, a cave-in at this mine fueled the Pueblo Revolt, which drove the Spanish from New Mexico in 1680. The rebellious Indians, vowing never to work the mine again, filled it and obliterated any sign of its existence. For whatever reason, the mine lay dormant for 150 years.

The treasures of Cerrillos were rediscovered in 1879 by two hard-luck prospectors from Leadville, Colorado, who followed rumors of gold into the little hills. They packed a few samples back to Leadville, where the assayer pronounced their find a bonanza. The rush to New Mexico was on. Within weeks, a thousand miners swarmed the hills, and by 1880 the mining district counted fifty-five mines producing mostly silver but some gold. Many of their mining claims stated that the new mine was originally an "Old Spanish mine." Three mines claimed to be extensions of the lost Mina de la Tierra.

Cerrillos was booming. The tent city blossomed into a real town with

An Old West town is exactly what First Street in Cerrillos resembles. The village has been used for a number of films—from 1959 episodes about Elfego Baca for the TV series *Walt Disney Presents* to *Young Guns,* featuring Emilio Estevez as Billy the Kid.

twenty-seven saloons, four hotels, a school, and two churches. One newspaper referred to Cerrillos as the "future Silver Queen of the West." Promoters brought prospective buyers in by train in hopes they would plunk down the $40 for a town lot. One hundred were sold in the first few hours. By 1890 Cerrillos had a population of 2,500.

The showcase of the mining town was the Palace Hotel, built by Richard Green in 1888. Green, who typified the enterprising spirit of mining towns, came to New Mexico in 1884. He and his wife, Mary, traveled from Texas in a caravan that included four covered wagons, sixty-five head of cattle, and eleven children. Green later used the wagons to haul ore from the San Pedro mines to the railroad hub at Cerrillos. For his family—topping out at thirteen children—he bought a seven-room house.

Green expanded his mining venture with the purchase of the Madrid Coal Mines. But his health failing, he sold the mining company and turned his attention to enlarging his big house for a hotel. The twelve-room stone-and-adobe hotel, built for $10,000, was a one-stop commercial enterprise. In addition to the sleeping rooms, thirty-two-seat dining room, and family quarters, the two-story building also included a tailor shop and offices for the town doctor and dentist.

Green died in 1906 and his wife sold the hotel in 1911 for $3,000, a price that reflected the economic times. A fire in 1890 swept through Cerrillos, destroying thirteen buildings in the heart of town. By 1900 the mineral-filled hills around Cerrillos were spent and the mines began shutting down. Its glory days over, Cerrillos settled into a quiet existence on the back road to Santa Fe.

Then in the 1940s, the timeless face of Cerrillos attracted the attention of Hollywood, launching Cerrillos's career as a stand-in western town. Most recently, Emilio Estevez starring as Billy the Kid shot up Cerrillos in *Young Guns*, while Bette Midler chased Peter Coyote through its streets in *Outrageous Fortune*.

Mostly, though, Cerrillos is a laid-back village of some 250 people and a handful of wandering tourists. Trees arch high above dirt streets and piñon smoke scents the air. The Clear Light Opera House, which dates to about

San Jose (St. Joseph's) Catholic Church, south of the village's movie set buildings, was built in 1922 and is nestled among old trees that shade the dusty streets of Cerrillos.

1891, is one of the few original buildings left—fire destroyed the Palace Hotel in 1968 and the Tiffany Saloon in 1977. Most of the "western" buildings on First Street are simply movie set relics.

St. Joseph's Catholic Church, built in 1922, has a tranquil beauty inside and out. Its domed bell tower rises above the trees, giving it landmark status. Its best feature, however, is inside. The barrel-vaulted ceiling is covered in pressed tin and painted creamy white, giving the sanctuary its uncommon if not unique character.

Lest Cerrillos appear too serene, the town also boasts a petting zoo, featuring chickens, llamas, goats, and pigeons, as well as a block-long trading post and mining museum.

Casa Grande Trading Post and Museum, (505) 438–3008

Waldo

Take Railroad Drive north from Cerrillos across the railroad tracks. Turn left at Waldo Canyon Road and drive past the Devil's Throne rock formation. The coke ovens are 4.3 miles from Cerrillos.

Waldo wouldn't be worth the trip but for its coke ovens. Named for Henry L. Waldo, then chief justice of the Territorial Supreme Court, Waldo never was much of a town. It began as a stage stop between Santa Fe and Cerrillos and later was on the Santa Fe Railroad route. In 1892 the Cerrillos Coal Railroad Company built a spur line from Waldo to the coal mines at Madrid. A few years later the Colorado Fuel and Iron Company built fifteen coke ovens in Waldo to process Madrid coal into high-quality coke. The ovens were used to "coke" coal, which meant heating it to drive out its volatile gases. The result was a distilled fuel that burned clean and hot. These properties made coke a favored fuel for smelting furnaces.

Although Waldo counted a population of 125 in 1921, its livelihood depended entirely on Madrid. Its ovens processed Madrid coal and its wells supplied Madrid with water. Some 150,000 gallons a day were pumped from wells at Waldo and hauled by rail in tank cars to Madrid. When the mines at Madrid shut down in 1954, Waldo closed up shop.

Today the town is marked by a few hardy cottonwoods stationed beside bare concrete foundations. About a mile west, a long line of coke ovens crowd the tracks, Waldo's lasting claim on history. While coke ovens at ghost towns such as Dawson and Koehler are reportedly more impressive, they are also closed to the public. Waldo's ovens, on the other hand, are in plain view from the road and, although a little crumbly, are just as historical.

A long double row of coke ovens, all open to the elements and badly deteriorated, line the railroad tracks at Waldo. Barely visible from the road, these brick ovens that once fueled trains running through the valley rise above the surrounding charcoal-darkened soil.

 Madrid

Madrid is about 27 miles south of Santa Fe on NM 14 and 3 miles south of Cerrillos.

A few years ago during a visit to Madrid, I locked my keys in my car. It didn't take long for my stupidity to attract the attention of Madrid's volunteer fireman, who looked like a cross between a hippie and a sheriff. When his attempts to unlock my door failed and he realized I'd have to wait for a locksmith from Santa Fe, he cautioned me "not to go wandering the hills taking pictures." Thus is Madrid—eccentric and a little threatening. Perhaps it's because the new residents of Madrid, the ones who rescued it from death's door, came here to get away from a prying society in the first place.

They had come, however, to a place that had been attracting attention for centuries. A family of Spaniards named Madrid mined coal here as early as 1835, and by 1869 a community bearing the Madrid name was established. (Madrid, however, is pronounced with the Anglo accent on the first syllable, MAD-rid.) The Madrid mines produced coal mostly for domestic use, but they also provided fuel to the gold-processing mill at nearby Dolores and, during the Civil War, coal for the forts at Santa Fe and near Las Vegas.

The coal production boom, however, dates to the coming of the railroad to New Mexico in 1878. The railroad expanded the coal market by hundreds of miles, and its coal-fired engines proved to be coal's own best customer. All the more so for Madrid. The Santa Fe Railroad not only acquired Madrid's mines to fire its steam engines, it also ran its main line just three miles west of town. By the turn of the century, coal production had become New Mexico's leading mining industry and 3,000 people lived in Madrid.

About this time, the railroad leased its Madrid holdings to the Colorado Fuel and Iron Company, which planned to use the coal in its own smelters. The company found, however, that because Madrid's coal deposits were in narrow, tilted beds, production was too costly. Suddenly in 1906 the company closed the mines.

George A. Kaseman, an Albuquerque businessman, picked up the lease, owning it until he was killed in an oil well explosion in 1938. His superintendent, Oscar Huber, then took over the lease and ran the mine. After all, Huber, whom some called a "benevolent monarch," had been doing just that all along. From 1919 to 1954, when the mines closed, Huber held a singular control over this company town.

Huber had the no-nonsense look of Harry Truman, a devotion to the Protestant work ethic, and a genius for public relations. His first challenge was to keep the miners happy or at least busy. For one thing, because Madrid's coal was found in narrow veins, miners worked in small, wet "rat holes," using only hand tools. For another, miners often didn't have enough work, especially during the Great Depression, when the mines were worked only once or twice a week.

Housing conditions at Madrid also compared poorly with those in other coal camps. Most of the miners' houses still showed the drafty cracks from where they had been sawed into sections and shipped to Madrid by flatcar soon after the turn of the century. Some employees, though, lived happily enough on the main street, Madrid's "silk stocking row," where their houses were better built and had indoor plumbing.

Huber solved the housing problem as he could, supplying paint, materials, and in some cases carpenters to repair the clapboard houses. Later he built a new section of town, known as "Hollywood," that featured indoor plumbing and electricity.

Huber also worried that if the miners had too much time to "grieve over

Business thrives on the main street of Madrid. Art galleries, coffee bistros, bed-and-breakfast establishments, and craft shops draw large crowds during the summer and weekends, when cars line the narrow highway through town.

their troubles," they might unionize. His solution was to create an Employees Club to which every miner paid 75 cents a month in dues. The Employees Club sponsored nearly every social activity in Madrid from Easter, to the Fourth of July, to its most famous event, the Christmas Lights. Club activities also included baseball, golf, and a spring parade that featured a marching band and some sixty-three floats.

These elaborate events often took weeks of preparation, using miners and their families as "volunteer" labor. During December a company-mandated Christmas tree was posted in every front yard, and 50,000 lights were strung from one end of town to the other. Trans World Airlines even rerouted flights so passengers could see the glittering "Christmas City" from the air.

While there was some grumbling about the "forced labor" required for the events, most everyone loved them. Not only did it give them something to do, it gave them a sense of community pride. And the union never got a foothold in Madrid.

During Madrid's waning days, most of the young men had already left for military service or jobs in cities, leaving the older men to work the mines. Courtesy Museum of New Mexico, #111691. E. W. Northnagel photograph.

These holiday events also paid dividends at the company-owned businesses. Huber himself supplied numbers showing that when employees stayed in town for the Fourth of July, profits at the amusement hall increased by a third. The Christmas display brought in thousands of tourists, who spent money on food and gasoline.

Huber succeeded in keeping the mines open during the Depression and World War II, but he could not compete with oil and natural gas, the new fuels of choice. Finally in 1954, Oscar Huber put the coal company and the entire town up for sale, including its 200 houses. For twenty years while the company searched for a buyer to meet its asking price of $250,000, the town dwindled to a handful of residents and 150 buildings.

Huber decided to sell off individual buildings in 1975, the height of the hippie era in New Mexico. Hippies were looking for cheap, out-of-the-way places to live, and Madrid's miners' cottages were going cheap—between $1,500 and $7,500 each. All 150 buildings were sold in sixteen days.

Madrid's reincarnation was evident almost at once. Within four months, its population climbed to eighty, and soon the town had a volunteer fire department, a cooperative school, and a single eight-party telephone line. Though some wanted Madrid to remain outside the pale, most of the residents hoped to sell their arts and crafts to passing tourists.

Nearly thirty years later Madrid had become what one resident calls "a haven for aging hippies." These days hippies run the thirty-three shops and galleries that are housed in miners' cottages, mostly along the old "silk stocking row." Gray-faced little cottages that once rented for $15 a month now come in chartreuse, hot pink, and Victorian green and sell for up to $149,000. The old two-story rooming house is now a grocery store. Both the former Catholic church and the school are now private residences. Madrid today has neither school nor church.

For all its color and creativity, Madrid still prefers its tourists in passing. While some of the back streets are marked off-limits or private, the main streets are entertainment enough. On my last visit, for example, I watched a cowboy named Dakota, a "freelance farrier," ride his horse up to the town coffee shop and order an espresso to go. In tribute to Madrid's past, the close-knit community of some 300 hosts a City of Lights celebration. The December event features a parade, carolers, live music, and llama rides. And in the spirit of Oscar Huber, merchants sell arts and crafts, not from the company store, but from their own.

 ## Golden

Golden is 11 miles south of Madrid on NM 14.

In 1828 a Mexican herder searching for a stray mule in the Ortiz Mountains happened to pick up a rock flecked with gold and heavy for its size. He knew it was gold because he had seen such stones before in Mexico. His discovery created great excitement and led to the first gold rush in the American West—twenty-one years before California's gold rush. The placer mines in the Ortiz Mountains early on produced half a million dollars in gold. Placer mining was a simple, inexpensive process that required as equipment only a flat-bottomed wooden bowl, called a *batea*, in which water was swirled to separate off the sand, leaving the gold settled at the bottom.

Of the several placer camps that sprang up around the Ortiz mines, only Golden is still in existence. Golden occupies the site of two 1835 settlements,

A survivor of the gold rush days of the 1820s and 1830s, Golden is a quiet village, whose gold can now be found in the sun-drenched grasses that climb its hillsides and decorate the graveyard of the church. Built in late 1830 to honor St. Francis of Assisi, it was lovingly restored by Fray Angélico Chávez, noted New Mexico historian and author, slightly more than a century later.

one known as Real de San Francisco and the other as Tuerto. At its peak the Tuerto mining district had as many as 5,000 miners and a village of 100 homes. By the late 1840s the mines had played out and Tuerto emptied, leaving behind only a small Catholic mission, built in honor of St. Francis of Assisi.

Despite a few small strikes, mining languished for decades, due in part to a scarcity of water. Then in 1880 the San Pedro and Cañon del Agua Company took over most of the placers with the aim of bringing water to the mines. To that end the San Pedro Company spent half a million dollars building dams and reservoirs in the Sandia Mountains and laying pipe from the reservoirs to the placers twenty-two miles away. In anticipation of the new prosperity, Real de San Francisco changed its name to Golden in 1879.

By the mid-1880s Golden, with a population of 400, was a commercial center with a bank and stock exchange. Golden was even host to former president General Ulysses S. Grant, who was on a grand tour of the mining district. Grant was so impressed with the San Pedro project that he agreed to be named president of the company, news that sent its stock soaring. When Grant realized the company was interested only in capitalizing on his name, he resigned and the stock crashed.

By then the San Pedro and Cañon del Agua Company already was in trouble. Its reservoirs weren't filling, and its pipeline was plagued with problems. Plus its claim to the entire mining district was in legal dispute. When the U.S. Supreme Court ruled against the company, it dismantled the pipeline and went out of the water business. Golden survived, but its days were numbered. By 1910 the mines had closed and Golden withered nearly to ghost town status.

Golden today is a collection of modern and ruined buildings scattered along both sides of the highway. St. Francis Church, built in 1835, still sits on its hilltop, its chalk white profile in stark contrast to the dark hills beyond. The church was carefully restored in 1960 by Fray Angélico Chávez, New Mexico's revered historian. The view from the church's cemetery to the west takes in several ruins, including the standing walls of the old rock schoolhouse.

Hagan

The dirt road to Hagan intersects NM 14, 2.8 miles south of Golden at Puertocito Road. Go west on Puertocito Road for 3 miles, then turn right at the fork that crosses a cattle guard. Hagan is 10 miles from the Puertocito Road turnoff.

The road to Hagan traverses a high grassy meadow, then curls down into a brushy canyon where a roadside cross, a *descanso*, marks a recent death on the hairpin curve. One arroyo after another cuts across the road, carving it into shades of rose and terra cotta. A sign offers land for sale on these "yellow hills and purple cliffs." To prove the point, the road passes beneath a cliff whose vertical folds look as if they were shoved straight out of the earth like so many pastel crayons.

As the road skirts alongside the Uña de Gato Arroyo, wide as the Rio Grande, the land becomes achingly more remote. Then on the east bank, like a lost city, sit the ruins of Hagan.

Hagan lived two lives, the first practical, the second full of promise. It failed both times, its fate tied not only to the fortunes of coal mining, but also to the vagaries of the railroad.

Coal was discovered at Uña de Gato, meaning "cat's claw," in 1902, at a time when coal production in the area was on the wane. Regardless, the

Autumn afternoon sun illuminates one of the two-story buildings slowly becoming a part of the sandstone ridge that curves around the crumbling community of Hagan, a coal-mining camp established at the turn of the century.

New Mexico Fuel and Iron Company, which developed the mine, pronounced the coal equal to any in the Rocky Mountains. By 1904 the mine was known as Hagan, named after a popular railroad official, no doubt to hasten the building of a railroad line to the newly named town. Mine officials knew from the outset that a rail spur would be crucial to getting its coal to market. In the meantime, coal was hauled by wagon to San Felipe, a siding on the Santa Fe line.

Work on the spur finally began in 1908 but was suspended after a few months, spelling the end for the mining venture. For a decade the mines remained closed and Hagan, which once counted sixty residents and a mercantile, lay dormant.

Then in 1919 along came Dr. Justin Jerome DePraslin, a "gentleman entrepreneur" out of New Orleans. Although Dr. DePraslin's title was questionable, his dedication to Hagan's revitalization was not. With charm and enthusiasm, he convinced investors to put up $160,000 to develop the Hagan Coal Mine. Plus another $70,000 for housing. Plus $216,000 more for mine buildings, including a power plant. And finally $300,000 for thirteen miles of rail line.

Forget for now that the investors never made a profit. Instead look at what DePraslin did with their money. In 1924 he hired master builder Abenicio Salazar and a crew of sixty workmen to construct most of the buildings at Hagan, including houses and a company store. True to DePraslin's sensibility and Salazar's skill, Hagan was an uncommonly genteel mining town, with a population of 500. The houses were built in the Pueblo Revival style popular at the time. And built to last—not, as their occupants pointed out, like the clapboard houses at Madrid.

By May of that year Hagan's coal railroad had been completed and was soon hauling coal, plus tile and brick, from the Tonque brick plant near San Felipe. Also, the old Hagan mines were being cleaned and retimbered. The power plant, constructed of red Tonque brick and reinforced concrete, was supplying power not only to the mine and town, but also to other mines in the area.

Then in the early 1930s miners hit a layer of shale that widened until they were mining more shale than coal. By 1933, the railroad, which was never profitable, ceased operation. Demand for coal continued to slide, and by 1939 the Hagan Mine Company had closed down. DePraslin's pretty town was dismantled and carted off.

Enough remains, however, for a visitor to appreciate Hagan's prideful history. The massive power plant, a lion in its day, teeters helplessly at the arroyo's edge, most of its foundation already tumbled into the arroyo. The remains of the mercantile, a back wall and rows of concrete pillars in the basement, outline a building that once was as fine as any in Santa Fe. Half a dozen small buildings on the hillside are Salazar's handiwork, although most of their adobes, "good and very hard," were scavenged by departing residents to build new homes in nearby towns. The sandy arroyo, which once provided the railroad its bed, gives not a hint the line even existed.

The once impressive electric power house at Hagan, undercut by the arroyo that slices in front of the old building, may eventually wash downstream after another century of thunderstorms and seasonal flooding.

Coyote

Coyote is 3.3 miles north of Hagan. The dirt road, which crosses several arroyos, could be hazardous during rainy weather. Definitely truck conditions.

Who in New Mexico has not seen a coyote? Watched it lope across open desert, its scruffy fur pale as sand? Or caught one loitering in town, hoping to snag a city mouse? Or seen its high-range cousin, big and gray, bolt across the road? This adaptable, intriguing animal the Aztecs called *coytl* and the Navajos named "God's dog" has lent its name to seventy-five places in New Mexico—springs, canyons, valleys, and a few towns, including one ghost town.

Coyote, Hagan's mining town neighbor, lived and died in the space of twenty years in the early 1900s. Founded in 1904, the coal town pinned its hopes on a railroad spur that would link it to the important Santa Fe line. But by the time the line finally reached Hagan in 1924, Coyote already was past saving.

The ruins at Coyote consist of a trio of buildings all in collapse, plus a few foundations crumbling on the hill. But with its windswept view of the eastern flanks of the Sandia Mountains and the wild arroyo at its feet, the hill is a perfect spot to watch for coyotes.

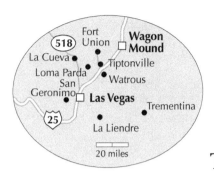

· 2 ·

The Santa Fe Trail:
Traders, Soldiers, and Settlers

Fort Union · Tiptonville · Watrous · Loma Parda ·
La Cueva · San Geronimo · La Liendre · Trementina

The summer of 1821 found Missouri trader William Becknell sneaking mules into New Mexico in an illegal attempt to trade them to the Indians. New Mexico was then under the rule of Spain, which in trying to maintain control of its colonies prohibited outside trade. To his good fortune, Becknell arrived to discover that Mexico, having just won independence from Spain, opened its borders to American enterprise. His venture was now sanctioned, indeed welcomed, under Mexico's law of the land.

The next year Captain Becknell forged an 800-mile trail from Missouri to Santa Fe, marking the first time wagons were used to freight goods west. Pulled by a team of oxen, each prairie schooner could transport up to three tons of merchandise. The steadfast oxen were not prone to stampede, a plus on a trail beset by Indian attacks. However, oxen proved tender-footed (they were sometimes shod in leather "moccasins") and were often broken down by the end of the trip. Later caravans used the more temperamental but tougher mules, commodities themselves in the Missouri mule-trading business. Season after season, caravans of twenty-five or so wagons rolled across the prairie. In 1843 alone, 230 wagons made the trip from Missouri to Santa Fe.

Santa Fe merchants bought goods from the Missouri traders and in turn shipped them south on the Camino Real to sell in Chihuahua, Durango, and Mexico City. These outposts of the old Spanish frontier—including Santa Fe—were starved for affordable merchandise. For example, under Spanish rule cotton goods had sold for $2 and $3 a yard, while the Americans sold better quality cotton for 31 cents a yard. The first traders reaped profits as high as 300 percent, but by 1826 profits had leveled off to a more realistic 10 to 40 percent per trip. The Santa Fe trade introduced American commerce to the Southwest, at the same time reinforcing the

18

Benito C' de Baca, whose ancestors established Loma Parda in the 1830s, gazes into the past as he explains the colorful history of this Mora River valley ghost along the Santa Fe Trail.

ideal of "manifest destiny," American's self-proclaimed right to possess the continent from coast to coast. By 1848, the American Army of the West had taken the Southwest from Mexico and the United States had laid claim to New Mexico. The "commerce of the prairies" now included freighters hauling government supplies to newly established American forts.

The history of that era still can be traced in the adobe ruins of Fort Union and in the crumbled buildings of Tiptonville, Watrous, Loma Parda, and La Cueva. Off the trail, other towns—La Liendre, San Geronimo, and Trementina—have their own stories to tell.

Fort Union

The exit to Fort Union is 26 miles north of Las Vegas on I-25. Take exit 366 onto NM 161 and follow it 8 miles north, where it dead-ends at the Fort Union Visitor Center.

Fort Union stands in the middle of a broad valley, looking like a sand castle ruined by waves. Only here on the prairie, a dry wind does this type of work. It is the wind Lydia Spencer Lane describes from her 1867 stay at Fort Union. It "whistled and moaned, and rose to wild shrieks," she says, "doing everything wind ever does in the way of making noise." Her husband, Colonel William Lane, commanded Fort Union, then the largest military installation in New Mexico.

By then Fort Union, built in 1851, was well established at the junction of the two branches of the Santa Fe Trail. The trail, which originated at Independence, Missouri, branched into two routes as it neared New Mexico.

The weathered walls of the hospital, located on one corner of Fort Union's extensive adobe ruins, no doubt witnessed a stream of soldiers injured and killed during their mission to protect area residents and those traveling on the Santa Fe Trail from attacks by Comanches, Kiowas, and outlaws. The fort was established in 1851 and housed as many as 3,000 soldiers.

By 1885, about when this photograph was taken, Indians often traded at Fort Union. In earlier decades Fort Union troops fought in several campaigns to subdue the Indians. Courtesy Museum of New Mexico, #37178. James. N. Furlong photograph.

Freighters could take their pick of either the Cimarron Cutoff, which traversed fifty-eight miles of waterless prairie and the dangerous territory of Kiowa and Comanche Indians, or the Mountain Route, which took a 100-mile detour into Colorado and south into New Mexico. This route posed its own hazards—boulders, ice, and a wild ride over Raton Pass.

By situating Fort Union at the juncture of the two routes, the U.S. Army fulfilled two purposes, each dependent on the other. First was protection of the Santa Fe Trail (and the territory's citizens) from Indian raids. To this end, the army established sixteen military posts throughout New Mexico. But because New Mexico's thin agricultural base could not support the nearly 2,000 soldiers stationed here, provisions had to be shipped in via the Santa Fe Trail, where Fort Union served its second purpose as the main supply depot for New Mexico's forts.

The first Fort Union was hastily built of unseasoned pine logs that just as quickly fell into decay. However, one army visitor observed that the "pine huts wore a neat and comfortable appearance." The first fort was abandoned in favor of an earthen star-shaped fort built nearby in 1861 as a defense against possible Confederate attack. Its barracks were so shoddy and insect infested that the soldiers preferred to live in tents. When this fort too was abandoned, the army built a third and last fort in 1863.

This is the fort where I walked one fall day, taking the gravel path that followed the fort's rectangular perimeter. Along Officers' Row, chimneys, corner walls, and doorways gave me a sense of life at Fort Union 150 years ago. Here were the commander's quarters that Lydia Spencer Lane described as being "built of adobe, and plastered inside and out, and one story high, with a deep porch in front of the house." Farther on were the huge storehouses, their tall adobe walls intact, where freight wagons were unloaded and their cargo repacked for shipping to frontier forts. The fort's operation required a skilled civilian force of wheelwrights, carpenters, and plasterers—all who were paid $65 a month—as well as laborers, who were paid $50 a month.

The one stone building, the cell block core of the old military prison, looked as if it still could hold a prisoner or two. The jail held the usual military offenders—deserters, drunks, thieves—as well as the criminal type drawn to a supply depot. One report stated that goods pilfered from the fort—300 pounds of flour and four sacks of bacon—were found at nearby

Army officers and civilians in front of the Commissary Office. Fort Union, which served as both an army post and a supply depot, was the largest military installation in New Mexico during the 1860s. Courtesy Museum of New Mexico, #160566.

Loma Parda, an off-limits village where liquor and women were the stock-in-trade.

The fort itself was not without its female population. In addition to the wives and daughters of officers and traders were the "laundresses." From my path, I peered into the adobe shells of their quarters, small squares of connecting rooms. Many laundresses were the "honest" wives of soldiers, while others were described as "complete terrors, a rough lot that frequently engaged in fisticuffs." For their laundry work they received $1 a month from enlisted men and $5 from officers. Some likely supplemented their wages as prostitutes.

In 1879 the railroad followed the old Santa Fe Trail into New Mexico at Raton and tracked south, negating both the need for the overland trail and the supply depot. The fort was abandoned in 1891.

Hounded by Mrs. Lane's shrieking wind, I gave a quick pass to the hospital buildings and headed to the visitor center and its sheltering storehouse of books.

Fort Union National Monument is open daily except January 1 and December 25. (505) 425–8025 www.nps.gov/foun/index

Tiptonville

Coming from Fort Union, the turnoff to Tiptonville is just past mile marker 24 on NM 161. Turn west on this dirt road and go half a mile to the first cluster of buildings, which includes the old store. Keeping to the right, follow the road about a mile to where it ends at a second set of buildings. The turnoff to the cemetery is .25 mile south of the Tiptonville Road on NM 161.

If you were flying over Fort Union and had just the right light, you could see strands of the Santa Fe Trail threading into and out of the fort. Even at ground level, the trail leaves its mark by shading the grass, where its ruts crisscross the plain. Some three miles from the fort, the Santa Fe Trail crosses the road heading south to Tiptonville, its wide swale a sign that heavy wagons passed this way.

In about 1849 the town of Tiptonville grew up around William B. Tipton's ranch, a few miles southeast of Fort Union. Tipton was the enterprising son-in-law of Samuel Watrous, himself a successful supplier to the military. As a trading post and traveler's stop, Tipton's ranch was perfectly situated on the north side of the Mora River directly in the path of various Santa Fe Trail routes.

Only a dirt road leads to Tiptonville today. Alongside the road tall,

Tiptonville, named for the rancher who founded the community in 1849, is situated along the Santa Fe Trail near Fort Union. Although most of the remaining buildings are overgrown with native vegetation, grazing livestock keep the shrubs and trees at bay in this section of the town.

arthritic-looking trees, bared for fall, are introduction to the tangle of bushes, briars, and thorny saplings that hide most of Tiptonville's ruined adobes.

The long Tiptonville store is roofed and used for storage, its owner living across the street. Along the back road are nearly a dozen adobe buildings, many hidden under lashings of vines and overgrown saplings. Out in the open, a cottonwood provides a glorious backdrop for an abandoned adobe house whose chicken coop and pigpens suggest the place has not been vacant long.

At the end of the road a whitewashed compound of several buildings was likely the site of the Methodist mission boarding school, built in 1869. The pioneer Methodist minister, the Reverend Thomas Harwood, and his wife both taught at the school, which served students from Tiptonville and Watrous. Fully half of the sixty students listed on the 1881 class roster had the last name of either Tipton or Watrous. The compound now houses a residence and a business. The school has been demolished.

The Tiptonville Cemetery, located in an open, sunny field off the highway, is the resting place of nearly two dozen Tiptons.

*Watrous is 19 miles north of Las Vegas on I-25, exit 364. The
Watrous Cemetery is 0.6 mile east of the Watrous ranch house
on NM 97 on the north side of the road.*

Two rivers with headwaters in the Sangre de Cristo Mountains join at a
place Indians and Spaniards called La Junta de los Rios. Here at the juncture of the Sapello and Mora rivers, travelers camped under cottonwood
trees, grazed their livestock, and traded with each other. In 1843, a group of
men, recognizing the area's potential, petitioned Mexico for a land grant that
had at its center La Junta.

Missouri-bound traders found La Junta a convenient place to join in the
safety of other caravans for the hazardous trip across the plains. One traveler

Cars and trucks traveling on Interstate 25 zip past this old mercantile and other east-facing
buildings on the main street of Watrous, an old Spanish village originally founded as La Junta
in 1868.

The Watrous school, clearly marked on one of the town's back streets, stands vacant and exposed to the elements. Pressed tin ceilings still grace the litter-strewn interior of the old building.

Samuel B. Watrous built his ranch house and store, shown here in 1885, at the confluence of the Sapello and Mora rivers. Courtesy Museum of New Mexico, #11605.

wrote that at La Junta in the summer of 1848, "there was scarcely a day which did not witness the arrival or departure from this camping-ground of a fleet of those prairie ships, the unwieldy Santa Fe wagons."

Sam Watrous, who had come to New Mexico from Vermont in 1835, bought a share of the land grant in 1849 and settled at La Junta with his wife and seven children. On a choice spot at the river junction he built a twenty-room hacienda, which served as both home and store. He raised cattle on his adjoining ranch, selling the beef and other supplies to the troops at Fort Union and to travelers on the Santa Fe Trail.

When the Santa Fe Railroad began laying track into New Mexico, Watrous and his son Joseph donated rights-of-way through their farms, plus land for a depot and rail yard. The railroad named the new town Watrous, relegating the place name La Junta to history.

By 1900 Watrous was a thriving business community that included two general stores and a hotel, barbershop, livery stable, lumberyard, slaughterhouse, and tavern. The town also had a Methodist church and a

Catholic church, a Masonic lodge, a school, and a post office. In April 1910, however, a fire started in one of the stores and swept through town, destroying nearly the entire business district, including the hotel. Spring winds carried the fire to many of the homes, leaving them in ashes. Watrous was never rebuilt.

Today the Watrous hacienda sits at the back of a wide green lawn, nicely framed by towering trees. The setting is still perfect, the house still impressive. The Watrous Cemetery is tucked against a rocky hillside on a side road not far from the house. Buried there are the five young children of Joseph and Katherine Watrous. Four died within a month of each other in the winter of 1884–85, possibly of diphtheria.

Main street Watrous is largely vacant but for Sacred Heart Catholic Church, which has been maintained. An American flag flies above the old wood-front mercantile, but its windows are boarded. One street west is the old livery stable, faded to gray. Farther up the street is the Masonic Lodge, decaying from the inside out behind its stone facade. Across is the school, a two-story adobe with bold architectural details. Its cracked adobe walls, however, seem hardly able to support the roof. But across from the school is the little Methodist church, sturdy in stone, with a big American flag draped across its entry. It is now a residence and seems happier for it.

Loma Parda

On I-25, take exit 364 north of Las Vegas onto NM 161. Go 6.8 miles and turn at the cattle guard on the north side of the road. Contrary to other accounts, the road is public, although it is not marked. Loma Parda is 1 mile down this gravel road and directly across the river.

Loma Parda has managed to be a thorn in somebody's side for nearly its entire history. Even today what little is left of old Loma Parda is passionately defended by Benito C' de Baca, heir to the Loma Parda legend if not the land.

Directions to Loma Parda took me over a surprisingly good, caliche road that curved down to the Mora River. There the road took a little dip *through* the river, then up and out the other side to become Loma Parda's main street. The bridge has been out since 1948, but its pilings support a rickety wooden footbridge suspended across the river. Barking dogs bring Benito out of his rock house and I holler for permission to come over.

He seems happy for company this bright morning and offers me a soda before leading me on a tour of his family's infamous old town. We head first for the cemetery and the graves of his grandparents and of his mother, who had died only two months earlier.

Loma Parda is situated on a bend of the Mora River where the stream curves close to a blackened shale cliff—the "gray hill" of its namesake. Settled as early as the 1830s, Loma Parda was at first a simple farming village. Before long, however, it became the headquarters for Comancheros, a mixed lot of New Mexicans, Texans, and Mexicans engaged in illegal trade with Comanche Indians. These illicit traders dealt in guns and liquor, for which the Comanches traded them horses and cattle they had in turn stolen from area ranches.

Of course, Colonel Edwin Sumner knew neither of Loma Parda nor its reputation when in the summer of 1851 he selected a site nearby for Fort

Once a place for soldiers to dance the night away with Loma Parda's lovely ladies, the old dance hall now requires careful footing over the fallen timbers, rusting nails, and mounds of fallen adobes.

Union, the army's main supply depot. What he was looking for was a place with water and grasslands and a place far from Santa Fe, which he called "that Sink of vice and extravagance." Fort Union may have been nearly a hundred miles from Santa Fe, but it was only five miles from Loma Parda. Soon enough, army officials were finding Loma Parda "a festering nuisance" and a "resort for thieves, murderers, and bad men and women of all kinds."

By 1870 Loma Parda had a population of 412 and could count among its many buildings a mill, a mercantile store, a hotel, and a church. Benito C' de Baca's great-uncle Toribio C' de Baca ran a regular taxi service to the fort, charging soldiers $1 per round-trip. The more frugal could take the well-worn footpath. Another uncle, Julian, ran the dance hall, where bands played in shifts twenty-four hours a day.

Residents of Loma Parda were defiant when the army declared the town off-limits to its men. For example, when two soldiers were badly wounded during an unprovoked attack at Loma Parda, the army demanded the civilian offenders be arrested. Loma Parda's official *alcalde* instead charged the soldiers with breaking the peace. Wanting to avoid an incident, the army sent a detachment of men to Loma Parda to arrest any soldiers violating the off-limits ban and return them to the fort. Instead, the brazen alcalde promptly arrested the entire detachment, holding them hostage along with the wayward soldiers.

When a lieutenant was sent to find out why the men were being held, the alcalde replied, "That is my business. I will keep them until I see fit to try them," adding that he would turn all the men loose "when I get through with them, and after that they can go where they damn please." The soldiers were soon released, and when they returned to Fort Union, the off-limits violators were arrested for being absent without leave.

The arrival of the railroad in 1879 rendered Fort Union obsolete, and in little more than a decade, the fort was abandoned. When the last detail left, Loma Parda lost reason to kick up its heels. Over time, the old families died off as their children left for the army or for work in the city.

Once in a while someone comes back, someone like Benito. He came home from Denver to care for his mother and stays to protect the town itself. He charges that ranchers tried to destroy Loma Parda, bulldozed the church, and allowed cattle to trample his garden. "You have to keep fighting for your home," he says, the glint of the old alcalde in his eye.

Truth be told, there isn't much left to save. A wooden cross is all that remains of the church, and McMartin's store is a three-sided ruin. Julian's dance hall is recognizable under a partial roof, while all that remain of the stable and "hotel" are low stone walls. Dogs, which Benito says are not his, climb over and around these old rock walls as if they owned them.

*The La Cueva Mill is 6 miles southeast of Mora or 25 miles
north of Las Vegas at the intersection of NM 518 and NM 442.*

If it were not for its simple history, the sound of rushing, tumbling water
would be reason enough to visit La Cueva Mill.

Vincente Romero was likely a beneficiary of the Mora Land Grant,
827,889 acres of pine forest and rich valley land, which was awarded by the
Mexican government in 1835. For by then Romero already was well established in the area, having brought sheep into the Mora Valley in the early
1800s. In those days, it is said he slept in caves and lived on fish from the
rivers and streams. He named the area La Cueva de los Pescaderos, "the cave
of the fisher people."

In La Cueva, Romero built a two-story adobe hacienda with high walls
surrounding the house and corrals. He installed a bell to warn residents of
Indian attack, calling them in from the fields to the safety of the hacienda.

Perched on a grass-covered hillside that overlooks the church and the rest of La Cueva, scattered
adobe ruins are a reminder of more prosperous days in the village, named for nearby caves where
its founder once lived.

Romero also engineered a irrigation system that helped produce great harvests of wheat, corn, and beans. When Fort Union was established in 1851, the foresighted Romero was well situated to supply grain to the fort. His mill, built on the Mora River in the 1860s, ground flour for farmers in the entire valley. Adjacent to the mill he added a large adobe mercantile. Romero's enterprise grew to include some sixty horse- and ox-drawn wagons he used to deliver grain to military outposts throughout New Mexico. In addition, La Cueva had a blacksmith shop, harness and tack rooms, stables, and shipping pens for cattle, sheep, and goats.

San Rafael Mission, dating to the 1860s, was built north of the mill and store. Like most Catholic churches built during the last half of the century, the mission displayed distinctly French features. San Rafael's French Gothic windows, for example, reflected the architectural preferences of Archbishop Lamy, New Mexico's French-born Catholic leader. Today the mission has

La Cueva mill, its water wheel busy only during the summer these days, was built by Vicente Romero on the Mora River in the 1860s to grind grain for area farmers.

been perfectly restored. Its Gothic windows and doors are trimmed in Taos blue and its steeple is painted bright white. Gravestones in the old cemetery across the highway west of the church date from as early as 1843.

When Romero died in 1881, his ranch and mill eventually were sold off. The mill's water wheel continued to generate electricity until 1949 and still turns during summer and fall. The old mercantile, now the Salman Ranch Store, is open year-round, selling raspberries from Romero's irrigated fields. La Cueva is designated as a National Historic Site.

Salman Ranch Store, (505) 387–2900

San Geronimo

Take exit 343 south of Las Vegas, backtracking to cross over I-25 onto NM 283. The road is paved most of the way. Take the left fork at 8.5 miles, turning onto the dirt road leading to San Geronimo another 1.5 miles west.

The road to San Geronimo stretches through a wide meadow heading toward the dark ridge of the Santa Fe Mountains. The car shudders in the gusting wind, while outside, a whirling windmill seems bent on throwing off its blades.

San Geronimo lies protected from the worst of the wind, in a little valley watered by Tecolote Creek. (*Tecolote*, meaning "owl," is a popular place name in New Mexico due to its mystical association with both wisdom and witches.) In the far distance is an iceberg block of granite once called Cerro del Tecolote. Today the high mountain is known as Hermit's Peak, for the reclusive monk who once lived there.

The village of San Geronimo was settled in 1835 as part of a Mexican land grant. The 400,000-acre grant encompassed prime timberland and lush creek-fed valleys. The settlement prospered as a trading center, receiving an added boost into the early 1900s from its share of the railroad business from nearby Las Vegas. But its prosperity faded, and soon after, most everyone drifted away.

Although San Geronimo today is no ghost town, it does have a slightly spooky feel, aided by the threatening sky. Abandoned buildings do their part. A log cabin along the creek crouches in the grass, while a wooden house on the hilltop is having its tin roof blown off. A house that once hid its rubble-stone walls behind plaster—neatly scored to look like stone blocks—is in the process of shedding its facade.

Occupied houses, adobe and otherwise, are in evidence everywhere, as are dozens of beyond-repair automobiles. Anchoring the village center is San Geronimo Church, freshly plastered and painted.

The San Geronimo Cemetery sits on the hill east of town. There the wind takes up its case again, bullying the grass nearly flat. An impressive black iron cross stands in silhouette against the pale gold grass. Over its shoulder, Owl Mountain floats on the horizon.

With a fresh coat of mud plaster, the San Geronimo Church remains one of the historic buildings in the small village that is not suffering the ravages of time. Old structures—several of them occupied—surround this church, climb the hill behind it, and cluster along a narrow dirt road to the west.

La Liendre

Take NM 104 east from Las Vegas for 7.9 miles. Turn south on NM 67 for 9.1 miles to the town site. The road is paved about half the distance, with a good but narrow dirt road the rest of the way. Use caution on the curves.

La Liendre was established as a stock-raising settlement in 1845. Today the ruins hardly resemble what must have been a lovely village on a bluff above the Gallinas River.

Why would people abandon such a valley? Here the river flows even in winter, and cottonwoods grow thick along its banks. In every direction juniper-covered mesas reveal their iron-based geology in swatches of pale rose and brick reds. Perhaps the scenery was not enough.

Judging by its remains, La Liendre once was a compact little village with buildings strung out along a single street. Betty Woods, in her 1969 *Ghost Towns and How to Get to Them*, described the houses as "built tight against each other." Its layout, in fact, earned it the unflattering name *liendre*, Spanish for "nits" or "lice."

Woods also noted one house with a Post Office sign above the door.

Pitched at a crazy angle, the wood-shingled roof of this rock building is barely connected and will eventually descend into the cholla-covered country of La Liendre, founded between 1845 and 1850 on a ledge above the Gallinas River.

(Liendre had a post office until 1942.) Among the buildings she observed were many under roof as well as a store and a "little crumbling church." Today La Liendre looks shattered. Only the store is under roof now, while a second building hangs on to the splintered remains of its roof. The adobe-and-rock walls of several buildings are in varying states of collapse, while the little church has lost its identity altogether.

La Liendre is taken over now by cholla cactus, which thrive in the shelter of every foundation. Evidently cattle also consider the ruins a rest stop on their way to the river below.

Trementina

Take NM 104 east from Las Vegas, turning onto NM 419 at the intersection. From the intersection, go 3.9 miles and turn right at the cattle guard. At a second cattle guard take the left fork. This road is gated but usually unlocked. The town site is a short distance from the gate. Trementina Cemetery is 4.5 miles from the intersection, just before the Trementina Creek bridge.

In Spanish colonial times the musical-sounding word *trementina* translated to an equally pleasing "pine trees." Trementina Creek was given this name, likely for the piñon trees growing along its banks. The name also applied to the Trementina Apache band that once lived along the stream.

Then in about 1832 Hispanic settlers established a small community—known as Trementina—on the creek's west bank. There they supplemented their farming economy by selling pine oil and turpentine, the distilled by-products of pine resin. Thus the word *trementina* came to take on the more specific meaning "turpentine."

The ruins of the original settlement lie on a bluff behind the Trementina Cemetery, which is on the north side of the road at the Trementina Creek bridge. The grassy cemetery is behind low stone walls. Headstones, tilted and rounded by age, are etched with hearts, crosses, and stars and are inscribed in Spanish.

Sometime around 1900 Alice Blake, a Presbyterian medical missionary, arrived in the area. Someone, possibly Miss Blake, led the effort to establish a new town on higher ground. Thus a second settlement, also called Trementina, was founded about a mile south. The energetic missionary later served as principal of the Presbyterian Mission School and as postmistress. She even inoculated the town's children against diphtheria, saving them from an epidemic that spread through the village.

A west-facing window provides an afternoon view of the many rooms in this buff-colored sandstone ruin in Trementina. Residents of the community, which still sprawls over a large area of a piñon-covered hillside, gradually drifted away during the Great Depression and World War II.

By 1904 some 200 people lived in the new Trementina. The town supported a store, church, hospital, and community house. All the structures, including some forty houses, were built of sandstone slabs without any evidence of mortar.

When Alice Blake's poor health sent her into retirement in 1930, Trementina lost its one-woman social service. Then drought and the Great Depression combined to drive its residents away to look for work. World War II completed the exodus, and Trementina emptied altogether.

The dozen or so stone buildings of Trementina, so expertly crafted a century ago, are a marvel even today. Wooden window and door frames offer picturesque views to interior walls and sometimes to the surrounding low hills. The church is recognizable by its sheer size, but the rest of the buildings are simply variations on a theme, except for Trementina Memorial Park, which is built inside the ruins and is the site of the Fourth of July Trementina reunion. The park includes a large covered pavilion and a set of rest rooms painted robin's egg blue.

There is yet one more Trementina—New Trementina. It's on the highway near the old WPA school. But it never had pine trees.

Trementina Reunion: www.trementina.com

Sugarite · Johnson Mesa
Ring · Raton · (72) · Folsom
Dawson · Yankee
(38)
Elizabethtown · Colfax · (25)
· Cimarron · (64)
Taos · Rayado · (21) · Springer · 20 miles
Wagon Mound

· 3 ·

Colfax County: Land Grant Legacy

Rayado · Cimarron · Ring · Elizabethtown · Colfax · Dawson · Sugarite/Yankee · Johnson Mesa · Folsom

In the last half of the eighteenth century, New Mexico's land grant conflict played its dramatic best in Colfax County. It had all the elements of good theater, including a stunning landscape, a larger-than-life cattle baron, and a gold strike. Plus two battles, one waged by lawyers, the other featuring a gun-toting preacher. And Kit Carson, briefly.

It is a complicated tale perhaps better understood after a short review of land grant history. To begin: For more than 300 years under Spanish, and later Mexican rule, huge tracts of land had been granted to favored citizens, sometimes as private property, other times as community grants. The free land was offered to attract settlers to New Mexico's great unoccupied frontier.

However, joint ownership of community grants later would create the most confusion in court. The court's dilemma centered on how to separate that part of the grant owned by individuals for their houses and small irrigated fields from the pasture and forest lands granted to the community as a whole. Also since there were no official surveys, grant boundaries often were vaguely defined by natural landmarks—a stream, a boulder, a tall pine. Over the long life of some grants, records became mired in conflicting information or were lost altogether.

The problem came to a head when the United States took possession of New Mexico in 1848. Under the peace treaty with Mexico, the United States agreed to honor the property rights of all New Mexicans. With that promise, however, came the requirement that every property owner prove his claim. The government assigned the U.S. Surveyor General the task of confirming title to more than a thousand claims.

At stake were millions of acres whose natural resources were as valuable as the land itself. Into this breach came clever attorneys, speculators, and an assortment of professionals such as the "experts in penmanship" who used

Hundreds of white iron crosses commemorate the coal miners who lost their lives in Dawson's catastrophic mining accidents of 1913 and 1923. The Evergreen Cemetery is the only cemetery in New Mexico to receive a National Register of Historic Places designation.

their skills to forge official documents. In the end only 6 percent of the land claims were confirmed as legitimate. As a result, Hispanic subsistence farmers were dispossessed of their communal lands, which in turn were either sold to ranchers or, in an interesting twist, became public lands. Even when claims proved valid, lawyers received generous shares of land in lieu of fees. For example, when Juan José Lobato's grant, dating to 1740, was confirmed, he deeded half of his 153,700-acre grant to his attorney.

One community grant that survived intact was originally awarded to Guadalupe Miranda and Charles Beaubien in 1841. It is best known, though, as the Maxwell Land Grant, named for the man who gained possession the old-fashioned way—he married Beaubien's daughter.

Lucien Maxwell's deal, which included a series of buyouts of other heirs, cost him $35,245 for title to the entire grant, believed to cover some 32,000 acres. His holdings eventually would total 1.7 million acres, taking up most of Colfax County and a slice of Colorado and making him the single largest landholder in U.S. history. (In comparison, Ted Turner today owns 1.1 million acres of New Mexico ranch land, a large chunk of it on Maxwell's grant.)

Today the Maxwell Land Grant is divided among many owners, including a state park, a national wildlife refuge, a national forest, and an immense Boy Scout camp, as well as its share of huge ranches. The old grant also is home to a string of ghost towns whose histories could not be told without mention of Lucien Bonaparte Maxwell.

Rayado

Rayado is 11 miles south of Cimarron on NM 21.

In April 1848 two fur trappers decided they were "getting old" and thought it was time to settle down and make some money. "We had been leading a roving life long enough," Kit Carson recalled of the decision he and Lucien Maxwell made to settle at Rayado on land owned by Maxwell's father-in-law. Carson was thirty-nine, Maxwell, thirty.

By then the two partners had accumulated lives of uncommon adventure. Carson, whose father died when he was nine, came west on the Santa Fe Trail at fifteen, making up in courage what he lacked in education. Carson settled in Taos, early on working as a cook and jack-of-all-trades. With Taos as home base, Carson eventually led fur-trapping and hunting expeditions throughout the Rocky Mountain West.

Maxwell was born in Kaskaskia, Illinois, and was raised in the shadow of his grandfather's successful fur-trading business. Tales of the rough frontier life fascinated Maxwell, who, against his grandfather's wishes (Maxwell's father died when he was fifteen), signed on with the American Fur Company and headed west. Maxwell's venture not only proved a financial success, it also put him in the good company of Kit Carson. In 1842 the two friends joined the first of John C. Frémont's famed western expeditions, with Carson hired as a guide and Maxwell as a hunter. Perhaps it was their reputation as toughened mountain men that convinced Beaubein to sanction the Rayado settlement. Beaubein, whose own son had been murdered by Indians in the Taos uprising, was well aware that the new settlement lay within range of hostile Apache, Ute, and Comanche tribes.

Rayado was established in a choice valley open to the east, along Rayado Creek and near a crossing of the Santa Fe Trail. Here Maxwell knew the upland meadows could support sheep and cattle, just as he knew the settlement would benefit from its proximity to the trade route. Within two years

Kit Carson died two months after this photograph was taken in Boston on March 25, 1868. He was fifty-eight. Courtesy Museum of New Mexico, #13307. James Wallace Black photograph.

some fifteen families had settled at Rayado, and Carson proudly reported the partners "were in a way of becoming prosperous."

Rayado's livestock, however, proved an easy target for raiding Indians. The settlers' appeal to the U.S. Army for protection resulted in the establishment of a small army post at Rayado. Maxwell, ever the entrepreneur, rented his house to the army for $200 a month, a gouging the commander endured until barracks could be built. Within a year, however, the army began closing its small forts, concentrating its troops instead at Fort Union, forty miles south. The army offered to station fifteen soldiers at Rayado if Maxwell would accommodate them for free. Maxwell apparently declined and the post closed on August 31, 1851.

Carson's adobe compound, then, continued to serve as Rayado's "fortress." When Charles E. Pancoast stopped at Rayado on his way to the California gold fields in 1849, he described Carson's ranch house as a two-story "log affair surrounded by adobe walls for purposes of fortification." While Pancoast said Carson's house "could not be described as stylish," he was fascinated by Carson himself. The legendary trapper, he said, was dressed "in first class Indian style in buckskin coat and pants trimmed with leather doggles."

The fine home built by Lucien Maxwell remains in excellent shape in the small community of Rayado, founded near the Santa Fe Trail in 1848 by friend and fellow trapper Kit Carson. The village, which boasts a museum created from Carson's renovated compound, is part of the Philmont Scout Ranch.

While Carson's compound was patterned after his adobe home in Taos, Maxwell's large house in Rayado followed a more American plan—pitched roof, bay window, open porches. Maxwell was no fool, however, and surrounded his house with its own defensive wall.

Despite their intentions to leave the roving life behind, neither Carson nor Maxwell stayed long in Rayado. The restless Carson joined Frémont for another expedition before moving back to Taos in 1854 to take a position as Indian agent. Maxwell left Rayado in 1857 for Cimarron, where he was in better position to engage Santa Fe traders and to supply beef to Fort Union.

Today the whole of Rayado has more the look of an upscale retreat than a ghost town. Carson's once crumbling adobe compound was restored by the Boy Scouts in 1949 and is now a living history museum. Just up the shady street is Maxwell's fine home, its protective wall long gone, its grass nicely mowed. Across from his house is Holy Cross Chapel, hemmed tight behind a white picket fence. Some three miles south of town the old Santa Fe Trail crossing has left a shallow, wide depression in the grass.

The area Pancoast described as "a beautiful valley covered in fine grass" still is. Only now it is part of the 137,000-acre Philmont Scout Ranch. The old scout Carson would have liked that.

The Kit Carson Museum is open to the public. (505) 376-2281 www.nenew mexico.com/counties/colfax

Cimarron

Cimarron is 47 miles southwest of Raton and 57 miles east of Taos on US 64.

Cimarron is full of stories. I heard a few myself while taking a tourist's stroll around town. Outside the old St. James Hotel, for example, a young woman on a bicycle stopped to offer me her personal hotel mystery. Seems she once owned rare photographs of the hotel, but they mysteriously disappeared. "Now the photos are on display in the hotel, but nobody will tell me how they got there," she said knowingly. Across the street, she pointed out, was where Maxwell's mansion used to be. "It's gone now," she said, and rode off, leaving me to stare at its replacement—a stark 1950s "ranch style" house.

The house that once occupied this property was built by Lucien Maxwell in 1858 shortly after he moved from Rayado. By then Maxwell was a wealthy man and owner of a vast land grant. Sharecroppers farmed his fields of corn and alfalfa, while ranch hands tended his livestock. Eventually 100,000

Ghost stories abound at the St. James Hotel, where the scent of roses accompanies the spirit of Mary Lambert, whose room is behind the sun-splashed window on the second floor. The historic Cimarron hotel hosted such guests as Clay Allison, Buffalo Bill Cody, and a host of others who contributed to the bullet holes in the restaurant's decorative tin ceilings.

sheep would graze Maxwell-owned pasture. In town his work crews built a store, blacksmith shop, barns, and several small houses. One visitor wrote that Cimarron reminded him of "descriptions I had read of baronial estates in Europe."

Maxwell, by then balding and sporting a thick, lopsided mustache, presided over a "manor" that took up an entire city block. His adobe compound included a two-story house with two separate wings. The east wing was devoted to family quarters, the west to socializing. The spartan furnishings, however, led one amazed guest to report, "The room we slept in was carpeted, but had not even a chair. However, in one corner there was a pile of wool mattresses from which the servants made beds for us on the floor that night."

Regardless, Maxwell's place was a favorite stopping place for old friends

Lucien Maxwell's house at Cimarron was already in a crumbling state when this photograph was taken. The east wing of the house burned in 1888, with the rest of the house burning down in 1924. Courtesy Museum of New Mexico, #147388. Edward A. Troutman photograph.

such as Kit Carson and for his sometime business partner Buffalo Bill Cody. In his "entertainment" wing, Maxwell, a devoted gambler, also hosted lesser characters to games of faro, roulette, monte, and poker, as well as the company of women.

It's a short walk from the hotel to Maxwell's remaining landmark—a three-story stone gristmill completed in 1864 at a cost of $48,000. The Aztec Mill is now a museum, but in its heyday the mill produced 300 sacks of flour a day. When Cimarron was selected as the site for an Indian Agency, Maxwell's mill not only produced wheat and corn flour for the Indians, it also became a supply depot for rations ranging from blankets to beef.

The mill story that intrigues me, though, took place on the third floor and involves Maxwell's strong-willed daughter and the Indian agency's military supervisor. Young Virginia, recently home from a convent education in

St. Louis, immediately fell in love with Captain Alexander Keyes. Virginia knew, however, that her father would never agree to the marriage, so she conspired to outwit him.

She enlisted the help of Reverend Thomas Harwood, a Methodist circuit-riding preacher, instructing him to come to the mill on Indian ration day since she knew her father would be distracted by the hundreds of Indians receiving rations. As planned, Harwood went up to the third floor just before 4:00 P.M. on the appointed day. Virginia Maxwell arrived at the mill shortly thereafter in the company of the miller's wife. The women climbed to the third floor, where they found the preacher and Captain Keyes waiting. Reverend Harwood performed the marriage, while downstairs Virginia's unsuspecting father was busy dispensing Indian rations. As Harwood recalled later, "No army general could have planned for a battle more wisely than she had planned for this marriage."

The couple kept the wedding secret during the weeks Captain Keyes

Built in 1864 by Lucien Maxwell, the three-story Aztec Mill serves as a museum of the town's wild past, where gunfights often settled the score during disputes.

In 1887 cowboys working for the Maxwell Land Grant Company delivered cattle bought in Colorado to stock the company's ranch in New Mexico, bringing the total herd to 30,524 head. Courtesy Museum of New Mexico, #5326.

waited for transfer to Fort Sill, Oklahoma Territory. When orders arrived, the couple left by stage, waiting until they were well away from Cimarron before sending a copy of their marriage certificate back to Maxwell.

Back at the St. James, the hotel staff treated me to hair-raising stories of ghosts in the halls, showed me bullet holes in the pressed tin ceiling, and allowed me a peek into Mary Lambert's room. There I swore I detected the musty scent of roses—"a sure sign," I was told, "that Mary's ghost is in the room."

Mary's husband, Henri Lambert, was a French chef who had served General Ulysses Grant and President Abraham Lincoln before heading for the gold fields in the West. In 1872 he settled in Cimarron, where he built a saloon that by 1880 expanded to become the St. James Hotel. From the outset Lambert's elegant hotel was a gathering place for celebrities and high-class outlaws. Zane Grey and Annie Oakley slept there, as did the likes of Black Jack Ketchum and Jesse James, who frequented the hotel's saloon and gambling rooms. For all its finery, the St. James was still a dangerous place. Twenty-six men were murdered there.

At least one of those murders was committed by Clay Allison, who reportedly killed eighteen men during his lifetime. The wild cowboy was excused of these offenses as either acting in self-defense or because he was drunk. He was known to ride through town nude, sometimes riding his horse into saloons. Allison, a zealous vigilante, once beheaded a notorious murderer, then posted the head in front of Lambert's saloon as a warning to others. Allison died not so peacefully at age forty-seven, when he fell from a freight wagon and the rear wheel rolled over his head.

Today the hotel is plush and polished to high Victorian. The old bar (with its bullet holes) is now a respectable dining room. A walking tour of Cimarron includes several other historical buildings such as Schewenk's Gambling Hall, the stage office, the Colfax County Courthouse, the Aztec Mill, and the 1879 Catholic Church.

Old Mill Museum, open daily except Thursday, May through September. www.nenewmexico.com/counties/colfax/

Ring

The turnoff to the Ring Place is on US 64, at the halfway mark (7 miles) between Colfax and Cimarron. It is marked only by a small road sign reading Valle Vidal 21 miles. At 21 miles, the dirt road becomes FR 1920 and it is another 9 miles to McCrystal Creek Campground. From the campground, the footpath to the Ring Place is an easy 15-minute walk. The road is closed January through March during the elk wintering and calving time.

At the heart of Lucien Maxwell's old empire are lands so splendid, they once were the exclusive domain of the very rich. Chicago millionaire William H. Bartlett bought 200,000 acres of Maxwell's grant in 1902 and built himself a "palace in the forest." Movie stars and business tycoons bought the estate in the 1920s, named it the Vermejo Park Ranch, and turned it into a dude ranch. Then in 1982, 100,000 acres of it, an area called the Valle Vidal, or "valley of abundant life," was donated to the U.S. Forest Service. Now anyone can go there.

I headed to the Valle Vidal in the fall, its most spectacular season, looking for an old ranch called the Ring Place. The road follows Cerrososo Canyon, where the thinnest of creeks slits the narrow meadow. On the far hills, stands of aspen are buttery gold against dark pines. Soon the road itself is hemmed by pines. As promised, the path to the Ring Place leads from the

Timothy and Catherine Ring's daughters are pictured here in about 1900. Standing are Mary, Margaret, Mable, and Maude. In front are Myrtle, Annie, and Amy. Four of the daughters died of tuberculosis before they were twenty-one. Courtesy Chambers Family Collection, U.S. Forest Service.

McCrystal Creek Campground, the way marked by a red-ringed photograph of Timothy Ring's seven daughters.

In 1890 cattle rancher Timothy Ring bought 320 acres from the Maxwell Land Grant Company for $960. Ring built a series of ditches from McCrystal Creek to irrigate oats and hay for his cattle. That year, the Maxwell company also sold timber rights in the surrounding hills, where a railroad company logged the forest for railroad ties.

Although the Ring Place was not large, his house was. The two-story house had nine rooms on the first floor alone. The top floor had six bedrooms, most likely for all those daughters. Since the Ring Place also was on the wagon road from Elizabethtown to Trinidad, Colorado, the house also might have served as a traveler's stop. But Timothy Ring died of tuberculosis in 1906,

and his wife sold the ranch back to the Maxwell Company. In 1937 millionaire cotton broker Benjamin Clayton leased the property from the company
and built a small cabin behind the Ring house.

"Mr. Clayton only spent one month here," says Margaret Laumbach,
whose husband, George, was the ranch foreman from 1937 to 1940. "He was
too busy with his business and the ranch didn't have a phone."

George and Margaret and their young children lived in the Ring house,
where they occupied the downstairs. "The living room had a lovely rock
fireplace and two big windows looking out to the west and south," she
says. "I kept a crib there, where my daughter slept in the winter because
it was warm."

Margaret Laumbach, a retired librarian, remembered her time at Ring
as almost magical. "When we lived there, McCrystal Creek was channeled
through the yard, so we had a grassy lawn and two big pine trees out front.
In the springtime, purple iris grew wild and it was gorgeous," she says.
"When I visited several years ago, I stood on the back porch and looked

This photo was taken in 1921, when Shorty Murray, far left, was the foreman of the Ring
Ranch. Next to him is Mason Chase of the Chase Ranch, Paul Nutter, an unknown cowboy,
and Willie and Walter Dunn. Courtesy Z. P. Ward Family Collection, U.S. Forest Service.

Boarded against the elements—and vandals—the Ring Place home commands sweeping views of the lush Valle Vidal and the Sangre de Cristo Mountains. Forest Service signs, posted on the walk to the old ranch and at the house, explain the area's history and provide a floor plan of the sprawling log cabin, which has nine rooms on the ground floor and six bedrooms upstairs.

out at those mountains and thought, 'Did I appreciate this that much back then?' But back then I had three daughters and just didn't have time to take in the view."

That view, all the way to Baldy Mountain, remains unbroken. Ring's big house as well as his barn have been stabilized by the U.S. Forest Service. Its employees often stay in Benjamin Clayton's old cabin. McCrystal Creek ditches still irrigate the meadows, home now to herds of elk. New-growth pines cover mountains once logged bare. A Beware of Buffalo sign—no kidding—is posted on the Ring Place trail. In 1996 media giant Ted Turner bought the Vermejo Park Ranch, kicked off the cows, and stocked it with buffalo.

McCrystal Creek Campground, www.fs.fed.us/r3/carson

*Elizabethtown is 5.3 miles from Eagle Nest on NM 38. Turn west
on the dirt road and follow it 0.3 mile up the hill to E-town. The
cemetery is on the next hill north and can be reached by taking
the dirt road that goes between the two hills.*

The debris of Elizabethtown's frenzied history lies scattered on a hillside
above the Moreno Valley. Two log cabins have fallen to their timbered knees,
spilling out their contents—a rusty stove, bedsprings, heaps of tin cans.
Across the valley, dark green hills stack one behind the other, higher and
higher, until Baldy Mountain takes the skyline at 12,000 feet. Gold discovered there in the winter of 1866 set off New Mexico's first gold rush and gave
brief life to Elizabethtown.

The discovery was inevitable. The end of the Civil War freed soldiers for
duty in the West, where they not only protected miners from Indian attack,
they also did a little prospecting themselves. So when Ute Indians came to
Fort Union offering to trade copper from nearby mountains, Captain
William Moore and William Kroenig quickly recognized its significance and
paid the Indians to lead them to their find.

The partners then sent three men, including Richard Kelley, to assess the
area so they could file a claim. One evening while the others cooked supper,
Kelley killed time panning for gold along Willow Creek. His idle hour—and
supper—was cut short when gold flakes glinted from his pan. He enlisted the
others to help, and each one came up with gold. With winter hard upon
them, they marked a "discovery tree" at the spot, intending to return in the
spring. By then, however, word was out and Baldy Mountain was swarming
with prospectors, looking not for copper, but gold.

Joining the rush were 300 soldiers from Fort Union plus scores of seasoned miners from the played-out gold fields in Colorado. One promoter pre-
dicted that New Mexico would be "another California." In the first few years,
the mining district produced about $250,000 a year, but in its entire history
it never produced as much gold as California did in a single year.

Since the gold fields lay on Lucien Maxwell's grant, he was in on the
boom from the first, joining with Moore and Kroenig in a copper-mining
venture. When their miners tunneled into the mountain looking for copper,
they struck a ten-foot-wide vein of gold-bearing quartz. During its first four
years, Maxwell's Aztec Mine produced $1 million in gold. Maxwell charged
the miners who worked claims on his land $12 a year rent plus one-half of
the claim's take. However, in a practice that would haunt his successors,
Maxwell rarely bothered to collect, and the miners rarely paid.

By July 1867 the Moreno Valley echoed with the hiss and buzz of

Using water under high pressure, miners blast the hillside to separate gold from the soil. The water was courtesy of the Big Ditch, a system of flumes that brought water to Elizabethtown from the Red River, forty-one miles away. Although the Big Ditch cost $200,000 to build, it resulted in $2 million in gold. Courtesy Museum of New Mexico, #148112. Aultman photograph.

Kroenig's steam sawmill running full-time cutting lumber for sluice boxes. Construction also was under way in Elizabethtown, which had sprung up on the valley's western slope. Named for Captain Moore's five-year-old daughter, Elizabeth, the mining town soon had 400 residents. Within a year E-town, as it was called, counted among its businesses twenty stores and saloons, leading one citizen to remark that E-town's liquor supply was sufficient to keep everyone drunk until 1870.

By 1870 its population had reached 800 and included a generous quota of gamblers, fugitives, and brawlers. Respectability eluded Elizabethtown even when it was named the county seat for newly created Colfax County. The handful of lawmen who ranged the region had to contend with lynch mobs and vigilantes who practiced their own rough justice. The case of Charles Kennedy was especially gruesome. Kennedy operated an "inn" some twenty miles from E-town, where his hospitality included robbery, murder, and on-the-spot burial. When he murdered his own small son, the boy's mother fled to Elizabethtown, where she revealed Kennedy's murderous ways. When it was rumored his lawyer might rig the jury, vigilantes broke into the jail and hanged Kennedy. The frenzied mob dragged his body through the streets, where their leader, Clay Allison, cut off Kennedy's head and stuffed it in a sack.

In the midst of the tumult, Lucien Maxwell in 1870 quietly sold his land grant, including his mining interests and his home in Cimarron, to a group of English investors. He retired to Fort Sumner, where he took up residence in a twenty-room building that had been the officers' quarters. The London syndicate—under the name of the Maxwell Land Grant Company—made his old home its headquarters, filling the rooms with imported furniture.

By then Elizabethtown already was on hard times. The rich lodes had given out, water supplies had become scarce, and the new land grant company was

Perhaps the most familiar of all New Mexico ghost town landmarks, this rock building in Elizabethtown retains its elegant lines even in death. Identified as a hotel by some and the town hall by others, the structure's original purpose has been lost—along with most of the remains of the gold-mining town, which boasted a population of 800 in 1870.

pressing miners and settlers to prove their claims or face eviction. Miners in particular insisted that their claims were on public lands and that their mineral rights outweighed those of the new owners.

In 1871 miners rioted in Elizabethtown, burning the home of a judge who supported the new grant owners. Squatters' Clubs, made up of miners, farmers, ranchers, and storekeepers, formed to fight the evictions. The violent standoffs, known as the Colfax County War, continued for nearly two decades.

The martyr in the squatters' cause was a circuit-riding Methodist minister, the Reverend F.J. Tolby, who had used both his pulpit and his pen to denounce the foreign owners. When he was killed on the road to Elizabethtown in 1875, his friend and fellow Methodist, the Reverend Oscar P. McMains, led a gang of vigilantes to avenge the murder. In their wake, they left three dead men, one by lynching, and a county in such turmoil that the governor had to call out the cavalry from Fort Union. Reverend Tolby's murder was never solved. As for Reverend McMains, he was found guilty of murder in the fifth degree and fined $300. The verdict was later dismissed on a technicality, and the preacher resumed his lifelong campaign against the Maxwell Land Grant Company. The war in essence ended with the 1887 ruling of the U.S. Supreme Court supporting the company's claims.

By then E-town was down to little more than 300 people. One visitor wrote wistfully, "It makes one lonesome to walk the streets of Elizabethtown. Although not an old place, it is deserted and, instead of the crowded houses, rum shops, gambling saloons, and hourly knockdowns of a few years ago, a sort of graveyard stillness . . . is everywhere."

Elizabethtown's brief revival around the turn of the century was halted in 1903 when fire swept through town, burning most of the business district. Still the town hung on until World War II, when mining in the Baldy Mountains finally closed down. The landmark that defines Elizabethtown today is the stone skeleton of a graceful two-story building of confused identity. The wooden building down the hill is likely Froelick's store. On the next hill north, the Elizabethtown Cemetery provides a spectacular view in every direction.

Colfax

Colfax is 28 miles southwest of Raton and 13 miles northeast of Cimarron on US 64.

Colfax is a drive-by ghost town, close enough to the highway to be seen out the car window. Stop anyway, if for nothing else than to contemplate its history of optimists.

The skeletal remains of a dining car mark the boundary of Colfax, a town that was privately founded in 1880 but whose promise of irrigated farmland literally dried up when big ranching interests diverted water from the nearby Vermejo River.

Colfax is one of the few towns in New Mexico founded by private entrepreneurs and promoted to the hilt. The New Mexico Sales Company thought two factors favored the new town site. It would be conveniently located at the junction of two railroads, and midwestern farmers looking for new lands to cultivate could irrigate from the Vermejo River, a stone's throw from the town site. They named it Colfax City after the county and in 1908 set out to solicit buyers.

They laid out wide streets and plated a thousand city lots, for sale at $40 each. The company representative, J.W. O'Brien, offered forty-acre tracts of farmland, of which he said they had a 40,000-acre supply. In March E.H. Fisher, the project engineer, told the *Cimarron News and Press* that farmers "can get water by driving wells on almost any portion of the land." Fisher and O'Brien, however, failed to foresee that big ranchers such as Charles Springer, Manly Chase, and John Barkley Dawson were developing a ditch system that drained water from the Vermejo to their lands, to the exclusion of the Colfax farms.

By the next January the company was sold to new owners. "O'Brien," the newspaper reported, "cannot be found by his creditors, who, it is understood, are quite numerous." Still, the new town persevered for twenty-five years. It had its own post office until it closed in 1921, its own school until its few students were sent to nearby Dawson in 1939, and a community church that never attracted much of a congregation.

By 1939, Colfax had a two-story hotel, general store, gas station, and about a hundred residents. By then even its old competitor Dawson was losing population.

Not much is left of Colfax today. What might have been the general store is now just a single adobe wall (with a dangerous open cistern near the foundation). There is no sign of the school but for a couple of foundations on a rise behind the store. The town is populated, though, by an interesting trio of railroad cars in varying degrees of decline.

Dawson

The turnoff to Dawson is half a mile north of Colfax on County Road B50, which is dirt but in good condition. Turn left at the sign reading "Dawson Cemetery, 5 mi." Dawson is closed to the public, but at the locked gate turn right to the cemetery half a mile away.

Dawson, New Mexico, in 1913 had the look of a prosperous midwestern town. Its public buildings followed the low-slung prairie style of architecture popularized by Frank Lloyd Wright. Architect Henry C. Trost perfected his brand of the prairie style, applying it to several of Dawson's buildings, including its fine hospital and the community church.

The 5,000 people who lived in Dawson in 1913 were mostly immigrants, Greek and Italian plus Mexican, Slavic, Austrian, French, German, Japanese, and Chinese. They lived in shaded neighborhoods called Capitan Hill, Five Hill, and Back Street in houses that rented for $8.50 a month. Dawson's four schools—and forty teachers—educated their children. They were proud of their high school sports teams as well as the fifty-five-member band. It was as near a perfect place as mining towns got.

By then John Barkley Dawson, the town's namesake, had taken leave of New Mexico and gone to Colorado to raise cattle, an enterprise he much preferred to mining. In 1853 young Dawson had gone gold hunting in California

The Dawson Mercantile, the biggest department store in New Mexico in 1913, boasted it had everything "from mousetraps to tractors." When Dawson closed, sections of the store were salvaged for building material in Raton and Trinidad, Colorado. Courtesy Museum of New Mexico, #9065.

but soon saw he could make more money selling beef to miners. His success led him to a partnership with the celebrated Charles Goodnight, driving cattle from Texas to Colorado's gold fields. One route took Dawson into New Mexico along the Vermejo River, which he recognized as prime cattle country. So in 1869 he bought a vaguely defined tract of land, some 3,700 acres, from Lucien Maxwell for $1,000. Maxwell soon sold the bulk of his remaining grant to English investors.

Dawson settled on his land, raising cattle and horses and forty-five varieties of apples. He used coal chipped off a nearby mesa to fire his cookstove, an innovation at the time. Soon neighbors were buying his coal. Taking note, the Maxwell investors, knowing the value of coal to the railroad, challenged Dawson's rights to the land. Four years and a U.S. Supreme Court ruling later, Dawson received not only confirmation of his deed, but a finding that his boundaries encompassed not 3,700 but 24,000 acres. The lawsuit behind him, Dawson in 1896 sold his mineral rights to the Dawson Fuel Company for $450,000, giving half to his lawyer, Charles Springer. At age seventy-two he moved to Colorado.

The Dawson coal fields lay in horizontal seams in the canyon walls bordering the Vermejo River. By 1913, Dawson's six mines, now owned by the Phelps Dodge Corporation, were producing more than a million tons of

Training for the Dawson mine rescue teams included a simulated disaster where formaldehyde fumes were pumped into a make-believe mine. Courtesy Rio Grande Historical Collections, New Mexico State University Library, RGHC 03150229. Carol and Dwight Myers Collection.

coal, making it the second-highest producer in the state. That year, Dawson also began earning the title as the "most tragedy ridden camp in New Mexico."

On October 22, 1913, at 3:10 P.M., a sharp crack, like a rifle shot, came from Mine #2. The earth shuddered and from below came a muffled roar, a great building force that burst from the tunnel in a 100-foot tongue of fire. Then black, oily smoke filled the air. Rescuers searched the mine for nearly a month until all the bodies were found—230 men. "As each body is recovered, it's placed on a wooden skid and drawn to the mouth of the mine by a mule," reported the *Raton Range*. "Some bodies are burned almost to ash. Others are blown to pieces by the explosion." Twenty-three survived.

Mining companies tended to place the burden of safety on individual miners and thus responsibility for accidents. The cause of the tragedy at Mine #2, however, was traced both to a careless miner and the company's poor ventilation system. Against company rules, a miner had set off a dynamite charge while men were still in the mine. Inadequate ventilation allowed airborne coal dust to linger in the tunnels. When the charge ignited the coal dust, it was like setting the air on fire. The fiery blast rushed through the tunnels, consuming all the oxygen and leaving behind a deadly mixture of carbon monoxide that suffocated its victims within seconds.

Phelps Dodge generously compensated the victims' families, paid for the funerals, and donated white iron crosses to mark the graves. Then it redoubled its safety measures. But a decade later disaster struck again. Carelessness and coal dust again shared the blame. On February 8, 1923, an explosion at Mine #1 blasted through the mine shaft, sending half-ton chunks of reinforced concrete flying across the canyon "like paper being blown to atoms," said the *Raton Register*. The gaping shaft then collapsed on itself, trapping all 122 miners inside.

Deep inside, Charles Cantalie and Filini Martini lay flattened but alive. Quickly they tore off their sweaters, soaked them in water, and covered their noses and mouths against the deadly gases. Twenty hours later the two, still breathing through their sweaters, stumbled on their rescuers. They were the only survivors.

Dawson never really recovered. By 1926 oil had replaced coal at the copper-smelting plants in Arizona. Railroads began converting to oil-burning engines, then later to diesel fuel. During the early 1930s, coal production dropped 72 percent. The 1940s brought wildcat strikes and a workforce gone to war. In February 1950 Phelps Dodge posted notice that it was closing Dawson at the end of April. Dawson's 1,200 residents met the news with resignation and shock. Credit to the company store was cut off, with outstanding debts deducted from the last paychecks. Medical services were

Most of its buildings dismantled and moved elsewhere, the Dawson of today consists of scattered brick, adobe, and wood buildings, rusting equipment, and corrals used for ranching operations. Every two years, the old town hosts a reunion for the dwindling population of former residents.

discontinued. Some families bought their company houses for from $50 to $400 and trucked them to Raton and Clayton. Phelps Dodge sold the rest of the town, from the coal washers down to the bathroom fixtures.

Today Dawson consists of a handful of unremarkable buildings hidden in the shadows of huge cottonwood trees. Once a town of 6,000, the place is now home to ranch hands minding cattle on J.B. Dawson's old grazing lands. In 1992, Dawson's Evergreen Cemetery was placed on the National Register of Historic Places, the first and only cemetery in New Mexico to receive this designation. Here among the crosses families come to pay their respects and to remember Dawson.

Lucy Kalec Tomchak, seventy-five, has stopped at the cemetery on her way home to Arizona. She was born in Dawson and lived here until she was twelve. "My father is buried here," she said. "I also have a stillborn brother buried here close to the mountain, but I don't know where."

Her family lived on Capitan Hill in a house overlooking the valley. "We walked everywhere, to school, to the company store, and to the sweet shop," she said. "These mining towns were like one big family." But in 1939 her father, a mining electrician, died of pneumonia, leaving a wife and five children. "There was no work during the Depression and Mother could not support us, so we were sent to the Croation Children's Home in Des Plaines, Illinois," she said. For five years Lucy lived away from her mother.

Then Dawson held one last tragedy for their family. "My mother, Alma, was driving to Dawson where she planned to leave a note at my father's grave, saying, 'Alma was here.' But she was killed in a car wreck on the way," Lucy said, close to tears. "It is great to see Dawson again, but also kind of sad."

Sugarite/Yankee

Take NM 72 east from Raton for 5 miles, then turn north on NM 526. The visitor center is about 2.5 miles north. The Ensign Mansion is on the right about a mile north on NM 526.

The Sugarite coal camp must be a favorite outing for school groups. I can imagine rambunctious fifth graders, with pads and pencils, taking notes at the interpretive signs, then rushing to the next stop on the trail. One group, I'd bet, would finish early and collect back at the visitor center soft drink machine.

Today, though, there are no fifth graders; there is, in fact, hardly anyone here at all. But I do have my notebook, and I take to the trail studiously.

By some accounts Sugarite was considered "the most beautiful coal camp" in the United States. Ranchers settled here in the 1800s in what was then called Chicorica Canyon. The word *sugarite* is a garbled Anglo interpretation of either the Comanche word *cocora*, meaning "wild turkeys," or the Spanish word *anchicoria*, meaning "chicory." In 1909 the Chicorica Coal Company opened three mines in the canyon. Soon high-quality Sugarite coal was in demand for home heating as far away as Nebraska.

By 1912 the camp was booming, with a population that eventually reached 1,000. Miners and their families lived in roomy houses made of coke block (akin to cinder block) and piped with running water. Railroad spurs ran from Raton to Sugarite and other area mining camps, easing travel and encouraging socializing. For example, the camp's baseball team rode the train from camp to camp for ballgames. And every fall, Sugarite residents cheerfully greeted the arrival of boxcars filled with grapes. Whole families participated in converting

Coal miners from nineteen countries lived in Sugarite between 1909 and 1941. Their company houses were built exactly alike and featured four rooms plus a basement, porch, outhouse, and coal shed. The company store is in the foreground. Courtesy Raton Museum.

these grapes into wine, a variety called "Dago Red." Sugarite also had a two-story school, a company store, a clubhouse, and a saloon. (Bawdy houses were relegated to nearby Yankee, which had eight.)

The trail from the visitor center passes at least a dozen foundations as it zigzags up the hill toward the mines. I stop for a shady rest at what was the company doctor's house, where he treated minor injuries and ailments. Interestingly, Sugarite has no cemetery. The highlight of the next stop is a stone oven in remarkably good shape. Here Italian Angelo Reccia baked twelve loaves of bread at a time, selling them for 15 cents each to Sugarite bachelors.

The mines at the top of the trail are not much to see since the entrances are blocked. Still intact, though, is the stone dynamite shack. From this vantage point, all around I see black hills striped in gold. These are mine tailings being stabilized with alternating rows of yellow straw. The straw is planted with oak and locust trees and rose, currant, and gooseberry bushes.

Sugarite schoolteacher
Leola Gates Sayr sweeps
the schoolhouse steps in
this 1915 photograph.
Courtesy Raton Museum.

Sugarite coal miners were
paid by the ton, not the hour,
and made the equivalent of
$12,000 to $19,000 by
today's standards. They had
to pay for their own mining
supplies, including miner's
lamp oil and dynamite.
Courtesy Sugarite Canyon
State Park.

A hand-forged iron door creaks on its hinges to reveal a compact dynamite building that guarded explosives used in the mines near the top of the mountain in Sugarite. The steep hike up to the building offers expansive views of the picturesque canyon and a glimpse of the narrow-gauge train bed that cuts into the forest.

The tailings date back at least sixty years, the last time Sugarite coal was mined. In the 1930s and 1940s home owners began using butane gas instead of coal in their furnaces. On May 1, 1941, the company shut down the mines. Many of the miners went to work for a rubber company in Colorado, others went to California, and still others went off to war. The company allowed people plenty of time to relocate, with some remaining as long as two years after the shutdown. Then Sugarite was dismantled and deserted.

In 1988 Sugarite coal camp became part of Sugarite Canyon State Park. Its old post office now serves as the visitor center. I had a soda there myself after my hike. Then I took a snooze on a picnic table, lulled by the cottonwood leaves rustling overhead.

Sugarite Canyon has one last stop—the Ensign Mansion. It's a forbidding place, hunkered behind a tangle of bushes. If it weren't on top of the hill, it would be hidden altogether. I was told the house was off-limits, first because of its dangerous state of decline and second because it is the haunt of mountain lions and bears.

Once, though, the Ensign Mansion was a showplace. A.D. Ensign was a Boston promoter who established the nearby town of Yankee in 1906. He chose Sugarite Canyon as the site for a guest ranch and built a luxurious two-story lodge there. He filled it with mahogany furniture, oriental rugs, and marble statues. It had plenty of bathrooms—five—and fireplaces—eight. The house overlooked a large apple orchard, where he planned to build a guest house.

When the mines at Yankee began closing in 1914 (old Yankee no longer exists), Ensign sold his guest ranch and mansion. The old house was last occupied in the 1920s. Today it is a weathered skeleton. Below, however, is the old apple orchard, still bearing enough fruit to attract bears.

Sugartie Canyon State Park, (505) 445–5607. http://www.nmparks.com

Johnson Mesa

The Johnson Mesa Church is 17 miles east of Raton on NM 72.
The cemetery is directly north of the church.

The road to Johnson Mesa passes through a valley thick with gambel oak in shades of yellow and brown. On the shoulder, wild turkeys cluster by the dozen, pecking at grass gone to seed. The road climbs out of the valley some 2,000 feet, then levels out onto a grassy tableland.

Johnson Mesa is a world apart from its downhill neighbors. Seven miles wide by fourteen miles long, the mesa was created by successive lava flows

Braving the elements of Johnson Mesa all alone, the Methodist church stands rock solid on this windswept plain that was named for the Texan who came to ranch and farm the volcanic land in the 1880s.

that followed the course of the valley, each one laying down a lava sheet from 100 to 400 feet thick. Volcanic forces "vented" through the molten surface, leaving behind conical hills of dark red volcanic rock. Even the wet-weather lakes that pockmark the mesa are volcanic in nature, the result of collapsed lava tunnels.

On this solid rock stands the old Methodist church, Johnson Mesa's simple landmark. A champagne sky warms its hard features—walls of sandstone and red lava rock—and gives its colored glass windows a cheerful glow. Visitors from nearly everywhere drop in most days, judging from the guest book.

For all its harshness, or perhaps because of it, those who lived on Johnson Mesa possessed a cheerful stoicism, beginning with Elijah Johnson. Following the cattle trails out of Texas in the 1880s, he came across the grassy tableland and pronounced it fit for cattle and crops. Others joined him, including miners who tried their hand at dryland farming, a practice that allowed them to work the mesa in summer and the mines in winter.

Since the settlers congregated at Lon Bell's place, they established a post office there in 1891. In 1897, the pioneers, predominantly Methodists, built their church a mile east of Bell's. For countless summers, the church was the center of Johnson Mesa social life. Once nearly 500 people attended a celebration that included speeches, singing, dancing (until 3:00 A.M.), ballgames, and horse racing.

When telephones were installed, residents shared the benefits. Five rings meant everyone was invited to listen in. On the line might be the Floyd boys playing the banjo, or somebody playing the piano, or someone else singing. Five rings also meant someone had a radio tuned to the evening news. This way all the farmers could hear the news and weather.

Eventually winters on the mesa proved too harsh and opportunities down below too tempting. Today a few families still live on the mesa, but none in winter. The church, which closed in 1943, has since been restored and is on the National Register of Historic Places. Services are once again held in summer. But in winter the Johnson Mesa Church is buttoned against the cold. Its windows are covered in plywood, and its pretty wooden door is protected behind a steel one. But it is still open. In the gray light from the door, the guest book shows a visitor every few days now.

Folsom

Folsom is 39 miles east of Raton and 20 miles east of the Johnson Mesa Church on NM 72. The cemetery is on NM 325 southwest of town, south of the road.

Summer is the rainy season in New Mexico, so when rain began falling at noon on August 27, 1908, people in Folsom were unconcerned. But that night, a cloudburst on Johnson Mesa sent water pouring down into the Dry Cimarron River. As the floodwaters swept toward Folsom, it tore Thomas Owens's house from its foundation, dashing it to pieces and drowning the family inside. When word of the disaster reached Sarah Rooke, Folsom's telephone operator, she stayed at her switchboard to warn the sleeping town of the oncoming flood. When it was over, seventeen people were dead and Folsom lay tangled in debris. Sarah Rooke's body was found eight miles downstream.

Until then Folsom had been a thriving railroad town of some 750

Home to prehistoric hunters 15,000 years ago, Folsom was a thriving cattle-shipping and ranching community toward the end of the nineteenth century. The old mercantile, which houses a small museum more than 100 years later, is one of the few original buildings that has not fallen into disrepair.

people. It was founded in 1888 at a horseshoe curve of the Colorado and Southern Railroad. The railroad camp was first called Ragtown, for its tent buildings, but when the first trains arrived, boosters decided the town needed a proper name. They chose Folsom, in honor of President Grover Cleveland's twenty-two-year-old bride, Frances Folsom.

There was reason for optimism in the early days. Folsom, a stockyard and cattle-shipping point, boasted seven saloons, two churches, a hotel, and a school. In 1899, it even had its own outlaw, the dapper Black Jack Ketchum. Before he took up outlawing, Tom Ketchum had worked as a cowboy at a ranch near Folsom, no doubt noting that the train slowed as it took the double curve south of town. At this spot, Ketchum would hold up the train not once but three times. The last time, however, the conductor was waiting with a shotgun. He shot Ketchum in the arm, stopping him cold. They took him to the Folsom Hotel, where the doctor patched him up. Then they sent him to Santa Fe, where the prison doctor amputated his arm. Two years later Black Jack Ketchum was hanged at Clayton. In a gruesome finale the noose jerked his head off his body.

Another cowboy, however, put the name Folsom on the map. Back in 1893 a black cowboy named George McJunkin, working on Elijah Johnson's ranch, noticed large bones protruding from an arroyo. Embedded in the bones were stone spear points. McJunkin, who had an interest in archeology, collected some of the bones, shellacked them, and displayed them on his mantel, telling his story to all who would listen. It wasn't until 1926 that his find attracted the attention of archeologists. When they excavated the site, they found the remains of twenty-three extinct bison. The spear points lodged in the bones proved that hunters roamed the area some 10,000 years ago. This prehistoric hunter became known as Folsom Man.

Although about seventy-five people live in Folsom today, Main Street has the look of a ghost town. The old general store houses the Folsom Museum. Empty are the train station, an old garage, and a row of storefronts overgrown with huge elm trees. The boarded-up Folsom Hotel, built in 1888, occupies a forlorn corner.

In the sunflower-filled cemetery outside of town, Sarah Rooke's grave is marked by a large granite tombstone, paid for with donations from 4,000 telephone company employees.

Folsom Museum open daily during summer or by appointment. (505) 278–2122. www.nenewmexico.com/counties/union

· **4** ·

The Rio Puerco: Village Life

San Luis · Cabezon · Guadalupe · Casa Salazar · La Bajada

The Rio Puerco looks long dead, its old course a sandy trench 140 miles long and in places thirty feet deep. The scoured riverbed is instead the mark of a powerful but part-time river. When the Rio Puerco does come to life, its waters rage downstream, where in a fury the river dumps its load of silt into the Rio Grande, then dies again.

Never good-natured, the Rio Puerco, or "muddy river," nevertheless once was better behaved as it flowed through pine and grassland and watered fields of corn and cantaloupe. At one place, the river skirted a series of volcanic peaks, knobs of black lava sticking out like sore thumbs on the tawny landscape. It was these lands that the Spanish governor of New Mexico granted to a group of settlers in the 1760s. Here they farmed and raised enough livestock to meet their needs, and here they settled into four villages—San Luis, Cabezon, Guadalupe, and Casa Salazar.

They occupied the villages sporadically for the next century, driven off time and again by the Navajo, whose own lands bordered the grant and whose raids sent the settlers to safer territory. New Mexico's Indian hostilities finally were brought under control in the late 1860s. When the Navajo Reservation was established in 1868, the settlers returned to the four communities along the Rio Puerco.

In their villages, they followed Spanish traditions dating back 250 years. They spoke the same language, practiced a common religion, and followed the age-old practice of subsistence agriculture. If theirs was a culture steeped in tradition, it was also spiced with superstition. Ghosts, strange sightings, and mysterious lights pepper stories told by old-timers.

Still, they never had more than a tenuous hold on prosperity. The Rio Puerco, unreliable at best, proved unsuited to irrigation and prone to fits of flooding. Rainfall, at about seven inches to ten inches a year, became a

Cabezon becomes a place filled with life three times a year, when former residents, their children, and grandchildren gather for mass at the restored church. Resti and Annie Sandoval, Max A. Tachias, and their families organize the event that brings old friends together in this picturesque, privately owned town on the Rio Puerco.

constant worry—and the subject of their daily prayers. Plus their livestock had to share the open range with a steady influx of sheep and cattle. By the 1930s drought and a deteriorating range led to calls for land reform, not only along the Rio Puerco, but throughout the West.

In 1934, Congress passed the Taylor Grazing Act, which for the first time regulated grazing on public lands. The legislation created grazing districts in which ranchers paid a fee permitting them to graze a set number of livestock on public land in the district. For the ranchers of the Rio Puerco, the days of subsistence agriculture were over. Economic survival now meant making profits and paying grazing fees. Many reacted by overstocking livestock on the permit holdings they could afford—a direct violation of the law's intent. When an attempt to create a special grazing district for subsistence ranchers fell through, their cause was lost. They continued their slide into poverty and eventually abandoned their villages.

Fifty miles east as the crow flies is another river town set in the shadow of another volcano. La Bajada, although older by a century and more fortunate in its choice of river—the Santa Fe—still shares a cultural heritage with the four villages of the Rio Puerco.

San Luis

To reach San Luis, take US 550 at Bernalillo. Go west 42 miles, then turn onto NM 39 at the sign for Cabezon and go 8 miles on the paved road to San Luis.

On the road west from Bernalillo my car plows into a spectacular winter storm heading east. The storm spreads a blanket of leaden clouds over all but the lowest sunlit mesas. Sleet bashes against the windshield as I turn south where Cabezon Peak pokes its knobby head through the cloud bank. It's a perfectly gloomy day for ghost towning.

Although San Luis is not quite a ghost town, what with a dozen house trailers showing signs of life and its no-name bar open for midmorning business, it does have the best ghost stories.

For example, there was the time a ball of fire attacked some mules. It seems one dark night a boy was riding a mule wagon past an empty house when "a terrible ball of fire" shot out of the house and rolled underneath the mules. The lit-up mules lit out running with the boy in tow and the fireball entangled in their legs. When neighbors later inspected the old house, they found no sign of fire, but once they left, the house lit up again with "sparks of fire" coming out of the chimney. They went back in; still no fire. Mischievous fireballs also were said to have chased people down by the river and to have bounced along treetops, lighting them up but leaving them unscorched.

There also was the mysterious hitchhiker who vanished, poof! from his seat beside the driver. And the time a man chased a coyote into an arroyo only to find the animal had changed into a Navajo woman in a shawl. Finally, there was the late night traveler who encountered a dark spirit on the San Luis road. The apparition, dark "from head to toe," crossed in front of the stunned traveler and disappeared into the sagebrush.

Notice that most of these stories were set in the dark hours of the imagination. But note also that the village lies in the shadow of Cabezon Peak, a mountain sacred to the Indians. And know that somewhere in San Luis,

Settlers along the unreliable Rio Puerco turned to their faith in times of drought, flooding, or raids from neighboring Navajos. The small community of San Luis is no exception. In addition to the well-maintained San Luis Catholic Church, a small morada and cemetery can be seen to the right of the church.

possibly near the Catholic church, is a *morada*, a "meeting house" of the secret Penitente Brotherhood.

The Penitentes take their name from the penances they practice—primarily self-flagellation and cross carrying—to purge their sins. The brotherhoods began forming in the late eighteenth century to fill the spiritual void left when Spain withdrew the Franciscan priests from New Mexico. In isolated villages such as San Luis, Penitentes served as religious leaders and village elders. Well respected, they also wielded judicial and political influence in the community.

Catholic reformers in the 1850s denounced the brotherhood for their excessive penitential practices and their political involvement. The reforms instead drove the Penitentes into deeper secrecy. In 1947 the church and the brotherhood declared a truce, which gave the church authority over the Penitentes but allowed them their penances in private. Estimates put Penitentes membership in New Mexico at between 2,000 and 3,000 in association with some 150 moradas. But nobody really knows.

In fact, I can't even find the morada in San Luis and decide to head south for Guadalupe. But the guys at the bar warn me not to go without a truck and not today. Outside the sky is nearly black.

Cabezon

To reach Cabezon, take US 550 from Bernalillo for 42 miles. Turn west onto NM 39 at the sign for San Luis, Cabezon, and Torreon. The road is paved until just past the turnoff to Torreon. Continue on the dirt road, which crosses over a large gas pipeline. Go 2.3 miles beyond the gas line and turn left at the fork. The gate to Cabezon is 0.5 mile east of the fork. The gate is locked, but you can view the town from the road or from a low mesa north of the site.

Every book on New Mexico ghost towns is sure to have an entry on Cabezon, the "big head." Authors have used their quota of words to describe Cabezon's setting, to review its history, and to mourn its passing. Photographers have done their part to document the tumbledown town, paying particular attention to the sad state of its abandoned church.

The story, though, needs a little updating. True, Cabezon Peak remains its signature backdrop, and certainly most of the buildings have continued their slide. But the church has come back to life, and people have come back to Cabezon—at least for today.

By midmorning small groups have begun to gather in front of the Iglesia de San Jose. Two men stand near the door, tuning their guitars. A group of elderly women unload from a van and walk quietly past them and into the church. Outside in the street cousins hug in greeting. An older man, wiry and tanned and looking a little preoccupied, makes his way through the crowd, shaking hands with some of the men. He takes off his white cowboy hat, then he, too, enters the church. He is Restie Sandoval, the mayordomo of San Jose de Cabezon and the man in charge of today's celebration. By the time mass begins, the church is overflowing.

When this church was built in 1894, Cabezon had achieved a measure of prosperity in its place along the Rio Puerco. By then the village had its own post office, three stores, at least one saloon, and a population that soon would reach 100. People lived simple, full lives. They planted gardens of chile and corn and collected asparagus that grew wild along the river. Hispanic settlers had occupied the area off and on since the late 1700s, living precariously at the eastern edge of Navajo territory. When the Navajo Reservation was established, the settlers returned for good in 1872 to the village known as La Posta.

La Posta, meaning "stage stop," was situated at the crossing of two old trails. The oldest trail had been used by Indians to travel from the Zuni Pueblo, south of present-day Gallup, to the Jemez Pueblo, just east of La Posta. The U.S. Army then used the old Zuni trail as a military route from Fort Wingate, near Gallup, to Santa Fe. The second trail, dating to Spanish times, ran from Albuquerque northwest to Cuba.

Although Cabezon (its name since 1879) was at most an overnight stop on the two routes, it also served as an early trading center for the Navajos. Rodolfo Tachias and Amadao Lucero each had a store in the village. However, it was a German immigrant named William Kanzenbach who recognized Cabezon's larger potential. He and a partner opened a trading post and saloon there in 1874. When they later ran into debt with their main supplier, the Charles Ilfeld Company, Ilfeld ended up owning the business. In 1888 he sold it to John Pflueger and Richard F. Heller. They paid it off in six months.

Their success was due in great part to their trade with the Navajos. Pflueger and Heller served as brokers for Navajo wool, in some years taking forty wagons full of wool to annual market in Albuquerque. In addition, they often took sheep in trade for goods. As a result, the partners soon had their own herd of sheep, 10,000 strong. Heller bought out his partner in 1894, the same year he helped build the San Jose church. In 1910, across the street from his fourteen-room house, he built a new store. Heller ran the trading post until his death in 1947.

By then Cabezon was at the end of its own life. The Navajo had long since taken their business to other trading posts. Grazing reforms in the 1930s had forced ranchers to compete for grazing rights, in essence shutting down subsistence operations. In the 1940s farmers who had depended on irrigation for their crops gave in to drought. The men went to work in Albuquerque or off to war. The women and children stayed for a time, but then they too left. The empty church was turned into a barn.

Restie Sandoval was born in Cabezon in 1929. Life then was good, he says. "We had no money, but we were content." Back then, farmers could irrigate from spring until mid-June. They built four brush-and-stone dams on the Rio Puerco to help raise the level of the water so it could be siphoned into irrigation ditches. But in the early 1940s a flood swept down the river, taking one dam after another. "When the first dam went, it caused a chain reaction that took them all out." By then every able-

Rising 2,200 feet above the town that took its name, Cabezon (Big Head) Peak guards what's left of this small community, founded in the late 1700s. The volcanic mountain was known as *tse najin*—"black rock"—to area Navajos, who believed it to be the head of a giant killed by the Twin War Gods.

bodied man in Cabezon was off at war. "There was no one left to repair the dams," Sandoval says.

Although Cabezon was deserted by 1950, it was never really abandoned. Today seventeen families own property in town. A few, like Restie and his wife, Annie, live there part-time. However, Cabezon looks every bit the perfect ghost town, looks that have created its own set of problems. Hippies moved into town in the 1960s, occupying the houses of absentee owners. "They moved into the house where I was born," says Sandoval, "and when they left, they hauled away everything down to the lamps." To protect Cabezon from squatters and vandals, in 1964 the county commissioner authorized the town to be fenced and locked behind gates.

Then in 1978, Father John Sauter, a priest from nearby Cuba, proposed an idea to Sandoval that meant only good news for Cabezon—restore the church. And do it in time for its 100th anniversary. "We had no money, no funds to do the job," says Sandoval. But they did have volunteers. Roofers donated their labor, someone from Rio Rancho came up with a potbellied stove, and a company in Albuquerque gave them a discount on the doors.

In 1994 the church celebrated its centennial with 500 people in attendance. Mass is held at the church three times a year now. Cabezon descendants come from all over New Mexico as well as from California, New York, and Virginia to attend mass and to honor the memories of their ancestors.

❧

When the last person has left the church, Sandoval locks the door and puts on his hat. He drives his truck past the house where he was born, past Heller's store and house, past a dozen buildings with a dozen owners. At the end of the road, he locks the gate behind him and drives on up the hill.

Mass is held at the San Jose church on the third Saturday in March, July, and September for Cabezon owners, their families, and invited guests.

Guadalupe

Guadalupe is 14.5 miles from the fork to Cabezon. At the fork, keep on the dirt road heading southwest for 4.8 miles. At this point the road forks again. Take the left fork, following it across the Arroyo Chico bridge. At 1.3 miles from the bridge, take the left fork on the road marked CR 279 to Guadalupe.

It seems much farther to Guadalupe than it is, a sensation I call traveling ghost town miles, where the landscape distracts you, roughs you up,

The old two-story home and store built by Juan Cordova provide a glimpse of Guadalupe's former grandeur before the 1930s, when a drought killed half of the livestock owned by village residents. Also, the dam on the Rio Puerco that was used to regulate water for farming burst, and the poor community could not pay for its repair.

and leaves you feeling lost. Then you come over a hill or around a bend, and there quietly, innocently sits your ghost town. And so it is with Guadalupe.

Although Guadalupe was abandoned half a century ago, its pale beauty looks ruined beyond its years. Its half a dozen buildings crumble in unison, walls pulling away, timbers spilling to the ground. Equally, everything in Guadalupe wears the same tawny shade of gold, from the bluff at its back, to the Rio Puerco at its feet—to the lone horse who ambles out to greet me. Suddenly Guadalupe seems the happy place it once was.

Juan Cordova's dance hall was as lively as any in the Roaring Twenties. Situated on the main road behind his two-story house and store, Cordova's attracted patrons from in town as well as from Casa Salazar, not five miles away. (Some 350 people lived in the two villages.) The neighbors joined in dancing to the music of the Tofoya brothers, with José on the accordion and Luis on guitar. By the light of gas lanterns, dancing began at sundown and sometimes didn't stop until four in the morning.

Weddings involved the whole community as well as families from nearby ranches. Nasario García's collection of oral histories about life in the Rio Puerco villages includes his own father's account of a wedding he attended as a boy. The elder García, also named Nasario, recalled musicians playing the violin and the guitar as they led the wedding procession to the church. "In those days the musicians rode a horse wagon in front and the bride and groom and the godparents [were] in another [wagon] right behind the musicians. And then the people on horseback and the rest of the wagons followed," he said. Afterward the men fired pistols into the air in celebration. It was like "watching a cowboy show," he said.

Dry as a bone on an early spring day, the monotone adobe buildings of Guadalupe melt into the earth in this once thriving village, which a handful of residents called home in 2002.

By the 1930s, life in Guadalupe mirrored the hard times of the nation. Drought hit the Rio Puerco Valley in the early 1930s, killing half the cattle. Then in 1934 Congress passed the Taylor Grazing Act, which regulated grazing on public lands. Ranchers reacted bitterly to the federal rangers sent to reduce their herds. "They came and humiliated us," one rancher recalled. "They threatened us that the cattle were going to die so we had to kill them and dispose of them. . . . The rangers themselves killed them. . . . It was a dirty business."

In about 1938, the log-and-brush dam north of Guadalupe burst. The simple dam had been used to capture stream flow in the Rio Puerco, raising the level of the water so it could be channeled onto the farmers' fields. The government, however, refused to help rebuild the dam, saying it was too costly. The loss was the final blow to their agricultural economy.

Like many villages and mining towns, the Great Depression and the draw of city employment drained off the population. In 1958, the school, the post office, and the store closed and the last family moved out of Guadalupe. But not for good.

Today Guadalupe remains the property of families descended from the early settlers. One occupies the schoolhouse, which has been remodeled into a home. One or two other newly plastered buildings also show signs of utility. Otherwise nothing has been done to preserve the village.

The church is recognizable only by its double doors, bleached the color of adobe. The roof has slumped into what is left of the sanctuary. Although the dance hall has been demolished, Cordova's big house stands as Guadalupe's battered landmark. While it still has all four walls and a rusted tin roof, it looks a little tipsy. The wooden balcony hangs by a few old nails, and its twisted tin roof dips dangerously at one corner.

The pale horse has nudged me out of my lunch apple and seems genuinely sorry to see me go. He has been a cheerful host, that horse.

Casa Salazar

Casa Salazar is 6.4 miles south of Guadalupe. The road should not be traveled during adverse weather. Flash flooding is possible following a rain. A four-wheel-drive, high-clearance truck is necessary.

The road to Casa Salazar begins its treachery about a mile from Guadalupe. There the road dips across the streambed of the Ojo del Padre, the "spring of the Father" that once provided Guadalupe its water and its original name.

Fiestas and high-spirited dances seem unlikely in the Casa Salazar of today, where a lone chapel perched on the edge of a mesa overlooks the Rio Puerco valley and scattered adobe ruins of this remote ghost town.

But concrete and old tires shore up the crossing, giving me confidence in the road ahead.

Whenever I've asked about Casa Salazar, people from around here all say the same thing—their mother, their grandfather, their uncles were from Casa Salazar, but no, they've never been there themselves.

Two miles ahead the road begins a switchback that leads down and through and out again from what my map says is the Cañon Salado. By the looks of it, the canyon just finished sending a boatload of water down this way. No concrete, no tires, in one place not even a road.

I've read that Casa Salazar once was known for its fiestas and dances, that 200 people lived here in 1880, when it was a "lively place." I read that women here would sew hundreds of tobacco pouches together just to make a tablecloth, that they dried pumpkin strips to eat during Holy Week, and that young girls wore embroidered aprons when they tended the goats.

Too soon the road plunges down a steep arroyo. My map says it's another canyon, but arroyo or canyon, this one is a wild ride. Rains have undercut half the road, forcing my big Ford to hug one side headed fifty feet to the bottom. Then its shift into four-wheel drive, take it up the other side and out. I'd have traded for a mule about now.

But the road levels out and I see where someone has hauled in a house trailer, setting it up at the base of the mesa. A couple of miles later the road ends at a gate. Casa Salazar—No Trespassing. On the bluff above, an old stone house is perched at the edge, taking in the view. Behind the house and off to itself sits a tiny chapel, its tin roof silvery in the afternoon light.

By 1905 Casa Salazar was down to a hundred people. In 1919 its post office closed and, like its sister villages, by the 1940s it had emptied of all but a few people.

If you should go to Casa Salazar, look up at the shining chapel on the bluff and say a prayer of thanksgiving for making it this far. Then say a second prayer, hoping you make it out again.

La Bajada

From I-25 take exit 264 onto NM 16 heading west for 4.1 miles. Then turn right and go 1 mile, turning east at the cattle guard onto a gravel road. Cross the bridge over the Santa Fe River, then turn left to La Bajada.

The village of La Bajada looks positively pastoral in its setting beside the Santa Fe River and beneath the black hill. In the waning light, a dozen cows cross the road, heading home. Like clockwork, the setting sun sends a rooster to crowing, which then turns the village dogs into a barking chorus. Sundown in La Bajada probably hasn't changed much in 300 years.

During Spanish colonial times, La Bajada, meaning "the descent," was a necessary stop for caravans traveling on the Camino Real from Mexico City to Santa Fe. Necessary because the "hill" behind La Bajada was a volcanic roadblock rising 700 feet above the valley. To make the hill, freighters had to transfer their cargo from the wagons onto pack mules. The mules made the climb with the empty wagons hauling up behind. The freighters reloaded the wagons at the top and headed to Santa Fe.

Coming down La Bajada—the hill, not the village—was just as troublesome if not more terrifying. In 1872, John H. Beadle, a reporter for the

Cincinnati Inquirer, found himself lurching down La Bajada. "Down the face of this frightful hill the road winds in a series of zigzags, bounded in the worst places by rocky walls, descending fifteen hundred feet in three-quarters of a mile."

Early twentieth-century travelers negotiated twenty-three hairpin turns on La Bajada, in the process boiling over radiators and slashing tires and creating something of a boom for the village repair shops. In 1932 engineers built a new highway, fives miles east of the old hairpin road, and the route of today's Interstate 25.

When the new highway abandoned the village of La Bajada, it withered to all but a few families. Its mission, which dates to the 1830s, fell nearly to the ground. Photographs dating from around 1975 show it as a roofless, hollow shell, in worse shape than Guadalupe's ruined church.

Brought back to life by the Montoya family, the mission at La Bajada retains its original 1830s design. The site was undoubtedly the location for the prayers of travelers passing through La Bajada, named for the treacherous descent on the Santa Fe Trail of 1,500 feet in less than one mile.

The interior of the restored church, prepared for mass by Pat Montoya, awaits visitors and the archbishop of Santa Fe prior to the annual late September fiesta in La Bajada.

The Montoya family, whose roots go back generations in La Bajada and whose homes surround the church, took on the task of rebuilding it. Eloy Montoya, a kindly man of eighty-three, says they "followed the same pattern as the walls" in rebuilding it. The result is a work of classic simplicity. So classic, in fact, that Montoya once came home to find a group of artists set up in the yard, painting the church. The intrusion angered the family, who are understandably protective of the property. He says they don't mind people taking photographs as long as they ask permission. "Donations help keep the church up," he adds. A little generosity is a small price for maintaining the one building worth seeing in La Bajada.

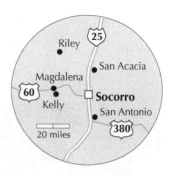

· 5 ·

Socorro County:
Rails and Trails

San Acacia · San Antonio · Magdalena · Kelly · Riley

In December 1878, the Atchison, Topeka and Santa Fe Railroad crested Raton Pass and chugged into history as the first train to New Mexico. The railroad followed the route of the old Santa Fe Trail but bypassed Santa Fe for Albuquerque, where it then tracked south. Here the railroad cut through the middle of Socorro County, following the easy grade along the Rio Grande all the way to El Paso.

For the towns in Socorro County, the Santa Fe Railroad meant immediate change, especially in the economics of transportation. The railroad meant that Socorro County's isolated mines could now ship ore to regional smelters. It meant that Socorro ranchers could give up long cattle drives and instead ship cattle out by rail. And it meant Socorro sheepmen could trade in their horse-drawn wagons for railcars to carry their wool to distant markets.

On its way through the county, the Santa Fe Railroad created the new town of San Acacia and revitalized the seventeenth-century towns of Socorro and San Antonio. The railroad made Socorro a major freight delivery point along its main route and built a branch line from there to Magdalena and a connecting spur on over to the mines at Kelly. San Antonio began to prosper as a business community after the railroad established a depot there. As a boy, Conrad Hilton met every train stopping at San Antonio, toting luggage to his father's hotel nearby.

Eventually, declines in mining brought an end to the branch line at Magdalena and its spur to Kelly. Riley, in the northwest corner of the county, lost its livelihood when mining and ranching no longer proved profitable. In the end, San Acacia's proximity to the railroad was of little consolation in the face of a flooding Rio Grande. San Antonio, once a thriving town on the railroad, is now just a lunch stop off the highway.

Schoolhouses and churches seem to fare better than other buildings in ghost towns, and Riley has hung on to both. The old rock school holds its ground in this deserted farming, ranching, and mining community on the banks of the Rio Salado in Socorro County.

San Acacia

San Acacia is 22 miles south of Bernardo and 14 miles north of Socorro on I-25 at exit 163. The cemetery is northeast of San Acacia across the canal bank.

The church at San Acacia seems not to have a name. I've been to many a ghost town church, and no matter how old or how ruined, somebody always knows its name. Perhaps that's why this church with its oddly placed steeple and its garden of weeds feels unholy to me. A white cross staked at the head of a narrow path gives me no comfort. Other paths, worn and recent, come from out of the bushes, all leading to the church. Inside, Jesus Saves is scrawled across one wall. In red. Who congregates in such a place? Not me.

Once I'm back out in the sunshine, San Acacia isn't sinister at all. The old school across from the church has been renovated into a comfortable-looking home. Its red tile accents reflect the architectural influence of the Santa Fe Railroad, from which San Acacia owes its beginnings in 1880. The town was named for a Christian martyr from Roman times—St. Acacio. In their carvings, *santeros* depict St. Acacio being crucified dressed in a Spanish military uniform.

While San Acacia's location along the railroad was beneficial, its position on the Rio Grande was not. Two wild and silt-laden rivers—the Rio Puerco and the Rio Salado—converge with the Rio Grande a few miles above San Acacia. In August 1929 torrential rains in these watersheds sent these rivers rampaging into the Rio Grande, flooding from San Acacia to San Antonio to San Marcial. A month later the flooded river struck again,

Nestled in the dense bosque of the Rio Grande, the community of San Acacia consists of farms dotted with a few homes and barns. This old church, overgrown and somewhat spooky in the late afternoon light, is one of the only remaining structures of the original village, founded to serve the Santa Fe Railroad, which ran alongside the river.

destroying all the crops in the valley and washing out the railroad bed. San Acacia and San Antonio were severely damaged, while farther south San Marcial lay obliterated under a blanket of sand and clay.

I am rid of the last vestige of gloom by my visit to the stark San Acacia Cemetery. It sits at the base of a rocky hill unremarkable but for one footnote of history. In April 1855, John W. Garretson, a government surveyor, chose this hill as the fixed point—the crosshairs—from which the United States would lay out New Mexico's survey lines in four directions. The boundary lines were used to certify land titles under the 1848 peace treaty with Mexico.

With this bit of knowledge, I backtrack through San Acacia's one shady street and without stopping head for the interstate.

San Antonio

San Antonio is 11 miles south of Socorro on I-25 at exit 139. Take US 380 to the intersection with NM 1, following this road south for 0.7 mile to old San Antonio. The Bosque del Apache is 7 miles farther south.

Piro Indians migrated to this lush, low-lying area some 700 years ago, where, on the Rio Grande's west bank, they established Senecú Pueblo. There the floodplain was fertile, and the "riparian thicket," the *bosque*, was full of wildlife.

Beginning in the sixteenth century, the bosque became a familiar stopping place for Spanish travelers on the Camino Real, the "royal road" trading route between Santa Fe and Mexico. After Spain gave up its quest for gold and turned New Mexico over to Franciscan priests, mission supply caravans followed the Camino Real to the northern missions. In 1629, the Franciscans established the San Antonio de Senecú Mission. The friars, who introduced many of the fruits and vegetables grown in the area, also built a winery at the pueblo.

In 1675, however, raiding Apaches destroyed both the Senecú Pueblo and its mission. Although the Piro Indians abandoned their village, its charred ruins remained a familiar landmark on the Camino Real for more than a century. Eventually, the ruins disintegrated beyond recognition and the exact location of Senecú Pueblo was lost.

The area remained uninhabited until 1820, when Hispanic farmers from northern New Mexico resettled the area. They named their village San Antonio after the old mission and revived the wine-making tradition. For

San Antonio—famous for the first Hilton Hotel, the ancient Piro Indian pueblo of Senecú, and the best green chile cheeseburgers in New Mexico—doesn't look like much of a ghost town except along New Mexico Highway 1, where historic homes and commercial buildings cluster near the road. The old Santa Fe Railroad depot rests there, among weeds on the west side of the highway.

the next half century San Antonio prospered as an agricultural village on the Rio Grande. Then in 1880, the Santa Fe Railroad, following the old mission trade route, established a station at San Antonio. Later the railroad added a ten-mile branch from San Antonio to the coal fields at Carthage. For the next fifty years the railroad served the mines at Carthage, including the Hilton Mine, which was established by San Antonio businessman A.H. "Gus" Hilton. The railroad stop was a transportation hub for the daily stages that ran between San Antonio and White Oaks, Fort Stanton, and Lincoln. Gus Hilton soon expanded his business interests to include the Hilton Mercantile Company, which also served as the local bank. Near the railroad depot, Hilton built a hotel, where he charged $2.50 a day for room and board. His son, Conrad Hilton, was born in San Antonio in 1887 and early on was put to work at the hotel. The future hotel magnate's job was to meet every arriving train—day or night—and assist the passengers with their luggage, all the while leading them to his father's hotel.

While mining and transportation were important to San Antonio's prosperity, most of the 1,250 people who lived in the area during the 1890s depended on agriculture for their livelihood. Most farmed or raised livestock, while others grew fruit, or raised bees, or made wine for a living.

By 1925, the mines at Carthage were no longer profitable and the railroad eventually closed its branch line. Then back-to-back floods in 1929 wrecked the town and ruined its agricultural lands. When World War II drew away its population, San Antonio never recovered.

The train doesn't stop in San Antonio anymore. The old Santa Fe depot sits in a grassy field, its long face turned away from the railroad tracks. Today anyone looking for the Hilton Hotel will find only the remains of a foundation on the southwest corner of 7th Street. Across the street is the former post office, now a residence. The Crystal Palace Garage, which has so captivated photographers, has lost its character under a thick coat of stucco.

A few miles south, the river lands—now the Bosque del Apache Wildlife Refuge—are as lush and as bountiful as they were when the Piro Indians chose this place as their home 700 years ago.

Bosque del Apache Wildlife Refuge, (505) 835–1828

Magdalena

Magdalena is 27 miles west of Socorro on US 60.

The old Bank of Magdalena is now a corner café specializing in "old-fashioned goodness." In the early darkness of winter, the brightly lit café has drawn a few loyal customers. At one table a Native American couple and their daughter are eating enchiladas on paper plates. Another family settling in at a long table hang their heavy jackets on the chair backs. The men nod a greeting to the other table while looking for a spot to stash their cowboy hats. Magdalena's wild cowboy days may be over, but it still has its cow town look.

Magdalena, however, owes its beginnings in 1884 to the mines at Kelly, two miles up the mountain. Due to the success of the Kelly mines, the Santa Fe Railroad completed a branch line from Socorro to the new town of Magdalena in January 1885. There ore from the Kelly mines was loaded onto railcars and shipped to the smelter at Socorro.

The branch line, in addition to its ore-shipping business, also gave Magdalena a boost as a stockyard railhead. In 1885 ranchers in western New Mexico and eastern Arizona rounded up their herds and made the first cattle

Cowboys string along the railroad tracks at Magdalena in 1885. Magdalena's stockyards at the end of the "Beefsteak Trail" were the largest cattle-shipping point west of Chicago. Courtesy Museum of New Mexico, #164502.

drive to Magdalena on what became known as the "Beefsteak Trail." The 125-mile trail, which ranged from a few hundred yards to five miles wide, traveled through forests, canyons, and the grasslands of the San Agustin Plains. Cattle made about ten miles a day, while sheep moved at half that rate.

The railhead at Magdalena was a boon for just about everybody, from miners and ranchers to Magdalena's merchants. By 1886 the town had a church and a school, plus a complete set of businesses, counting one bookstore and four saloons. One resident reported that "the town is very orderly at present, but generally keeps up its reputation as a frontier town."

For that, Magdalena could thank the cowboys working the cattle drives, which sometimes brought as many as 100,000 head of sheep and cattle at a time to the railhead. With their work completed, trail-riding cowboys patronized Magdalena's saloons and brothels. Cowboys often ended a night's spree by racing their horses along Main Street's boardwalk. Then near the depot they would jump their horses off the high end of the boardwalk, shooting their guns into the air.

Such was Magdalena in 1886 as described by Agnes Morley Cleaveland in her book *No Life for a Lady*. Upon their arrival, her mother instructed the hotel clerk: "Please give me a room that is not directly over the barroom. I'm afraid those bullets will come up through the floor."

In 1897 Magdalena also began shipping wool to eastern markets. That year, Solomon Luna, the territory's largest sheep rancher, arrived in town, leading a string of wagons loaded with wool. At the depot, he piled the bags of wool on the ground, then left two men with carbines to guard the pile while he went back for a second load. By the next season, Magdalena had a wool warehouse. There ranchers stored their wool until the end of the season, when the wool was auctioned and shipped to bidders as far away as Boston. Later the Charles Ilfeld Company, one of New Mexico's largest mercantile companies, also built a warehouse near the railroad depot. Ilfeld's Warehouse sold supplies on credit to ranchers, who settled up their bills after their cattle sold in the fall.

By the turn of the century, the fine brick buildings in Magdalena's business district were proof of its continued prosperity. By 1908 the Bank of Magdalena

Small residents, eager to pose for the camera in the fading afternoon light, are dwarfed by their home, Magdalena's massive Hall Hotel, which was constructed in 1917. The community sprang to life with the coming of the railroad in 1884 and supported the nearby mining town of Kelly as well as ranchers shipping their cattle to distant markets.

had been established on a Main Street corner, and 1911 saw construction of the Salome Store and Warehouse. The three-story Hall Hotel—with walls three bricks thick—opened in 1917. By 1919 Magdalena had a new grade school and high school, both designed by the well-known El Paso architectural firm of Trost & Trost.

Then in 1929 the Bank of Magdalena failed. In the 1930s a saturated cattle market and drought took their toll. When the government established a wool warehouse in Albuquerque, offering cut rates to wool growers, ranchers loaded their wool on trucks and headed straight to Albuquerque. Magdalena's warehouses were left empty. By 1960 trucks also had replaced the "Beefsteak Trail" for taking livestock to market. In 1972, the railroad abandoned its Magdalena branch line. By then, fires had destroyed 80 percent of Magdalena's old business district.

Regardless, there is still much to see in Magdalena, a town of some 1,000 people. Among its nearly two dozen historical buildings are the depot, now a cozy library that calls itself "The Reading Room at the Trail's End," and its neighbor, the Boxcar Museum. Across the street, Ilfeld's Warehouse is still in operation, while the Hall Hotel has been renovated into apartments. Visitors looking for a taste of cowboy days can take in a London Frontier Theatre Company production showing at the 1936 WPA gymnasium.

Boxcar Museum. Donation. www.magdalena-nm.com

Kelly

In Magdalena turn south off US 60 near the Ranger Station and go 1.9 miles, then take the left fork at the sign for Kelly. Park at the church and walk east to the mine gate. The Kelly Cemetery is directly north of the church a short way up a dirt road.

When Muriel Siebell Wolle visited Kelly in 1952, Main Street was lined with ruined adobe buildings. "No roofs remained," she wrote in her book *The Bonanza Trail*, "only crumbling walls with gaping holes where doors and windows had been." On the side streets she found a few frame houses with porches smothered in vines. "Debris was strewn everywhere, rusty, rattling sheets of corrugated iron, old bed springs, broken fences, and cellar excavations filled with trash." Wolle was so captivated by Kelly's fallen-down state that she gave it first mention in her book on western ghost towns.

Kelly also was blessed by its mythical setting in the shadow of Magdalena Peak. Legend has it that in the 1540s a small party of Spanish soldiers being

Remnants from Kelly's mining past—the head frame and towering smelter oven of the Kelly mine—are perched high above the town site of this community that excavated zinc, lead, and silver worth millions of dollars during its boom years.

pursued by Indians took refuge at the base of the peak. On the mountain's east slope, they saw a woman's face outlined in the rocks and shrubs. The features reminded them of a similar mountain in Spain where following the death of Mary Magdalene her face miraculously appeared carved into the stone. From this legend grew the belief that Magdalena Peak offered white men protection from the Indians.

For the next 300 years, however, white men left the mountains to the Indians. Then in 1863, a Union soldier named Pete Kinsinger was on duty in the area (and prospecting on the side) when he found silver ore near the mountain. After the Civil War he headed for the silver strikes at Elizabethtown and there told Colonel J.S. Hutchason about his find at Magdalena. Kinsinger stayed on to try his luck at E-town, but Hutchason left for the Magdalena Mountains. In the spring of 1866 he found three limestone outcroppings that would become the future locations of the Juanita, Graphic, and Kelly mines.

He first worked the Juanita and Graphic claims, mining oxidized lead-zinc ore. Hutchason smelted the ore in a crude adobe furnace he built on the site. Smelting reduced the raw ore into compact lead bars, called "pigs," which he then shipped by oxcart across the Santa Fe Trail to Kansas City. He took on a partner, Andy Kelly, to work the third claim. Kelly gave the claim his name, but when he failed to do the work required to retain it, Hutchason jumped the claim, taking it for himself. The Kelly Mine produced a rich ore averaging 50 to 60 percent lead and ten ounces of silver per ton.

News of Hutchason's one-two-three strike brought so many prospectors to the area that in 1870, miners laid out a town site and named it Kelly—not for Andy, but for the successful mine. In 1876 Hutchason began divesting himself of his mines. First he leased out the Juanita Mine, then sold the Graphic Mine for $30,000. He also sold the Kelly Mine to Gustav Billings for $45,000.

Billings, who had earned a fortune from his smelter in Leadville, Colorado, built a smelter in Socorro in 1883 to process the silver and lead-bearing ore from the Kelly Mine as well as from other mines in the region. Within a few months, the Socorro smelter had shipped 185 carloads of bullion out on the

The building with the skylight may have been Joseph Smith's photography studio in Kelly. The glass panes on the roof would have provided sufficient light for indoor photography. Courtesy Rio Grande Historical Collections, New Mexico State University Library, RG95-128.

Santa Fe Railroad. With this success, Billings persuaded the railroad to build a branch to Magdalena and a two-mile spur on to Kelly in 1885.

Blessed by the good fortunes of the railroad and the mines, Kelly seemed unstoppable. On the one hand, it had two churches, three stores, and a couple of hotels, while on the other hand, it had seven saloons and a couple of dance halls that stayed open all night. Kelly soon was so crowded that the hotels began renting beds in three eight-hour shifts, with customers limited to no more than one shift a night.

Kelly's wild ride slowed in 1893, when the devaluation of silver closed mines throughout the West. That year, Billings shut down his Socorro smelter. Still, the Kelly mines kept producing lead and zinc. By 1904, the mines at Kelly had produced $8.7 million in lead-silver ore, and Kelly was reaching a population of 3,000.

With a view for eternity, former residents of Kelly rest in a peaceful hillside cemetery that overlooks Magdalena Peak, which was sacred to the region's American Indians and the transient Spaniards who named it in honor of Mary Magdalene.

By then, Kelly was into its second boom. In the 1890s Cony T. Brown, a self-taught geologist and successful businessman from Socorro, had taken note of the greenish rocks at the Graphic Mine dump. When he had the rock assayed, he discovered it was valuable zinc carbonate, called smithsonite, a pigment used in paints and coatings. Brown and his partner, J.B. Fitch, immediately leased all the mine dumps, as well as all available mine properties. In 1904, they sold the Graphic Mine to the Sherwin-Williams Paint Company for $150,000. That year, Gustav Billings sold the Kelly Mine to the Tri-Bullion Smelting and Development Company for $200,000. Between 1904 and 1928, Kelly was the leading zinc producer in the state, with its total mineral output during that period worth more than $21 million.

By the end of the 1920s, Kelly's second boom had ended. The zinc mines were nearly exhausted. Only one carload of smithsonite was shipped in all of 1931. By the time Wolle made her ghost town visit, two families remained in Kelly.

Today Kelly has been stripped of its ruined adobes and rusted bedsprings. Only the church and a few concrete foundations mark Main Street. The Kelly Mine, with its head frame and brick smelter ovens, stands tall against the mountain and still seems operational. The prettiest spot in Kelly these days is the cemetery. The steep hillside harbors dozens of family plots, each protected by a fence, each within the protective gaze of Magdalena on the opposite mountain.

The Kelly Mine is open for tours on summer weekends. www.magdalena-nm .com

Riley

Riley is 21 miles north of Magdalena on FR 354, which is a good dirt road. Take the first turnoff north of the Magdalena Depot Library. The only caution is in crossing the Rio Salado at Riley. The riverbed is easily forded, but you also can park on the west bank and walk over to Riley. Riley also can be reached from I-25 at the Bernardo exit. At the end of this 32-mile route, however, you must cross the Rio Salado twice.

Outside, the blue-gray morning was still as ice. But by the time I get on the road, the sun has burned away the clouds, promising a clear, cold day ahead. The road to Riley takes me through the Cibola National Forest, where it skirts alongside the Bear Mountains. Its brown-sugar foothills are covered in a stubble of low juniper.

Late summer clouds drift over the numerous old adobe buildings of Riley, a picturesque ghost town that was settled in 1880 and once inhabited by 150 people during its mining heyday.

As the road veers away from the mountains, it opens onto a panorama dominated by Ladron Peak, "Thieves" Mountain. Suddenly a forest of yucca trees fills the landscape, then refuses to grow past an unseen boundary farther on. Even the roadbed is a natural wonder, here showing bands of yellow ochre, ahead turning shades of mauve and rose.

Closer to Riley, everything takes on a rough sameness, brown and barren. At the Rio Salado, true to its name, "salty river," the riverbank is rimmed in white, encrusted bank to bank in a thin residue of salt. Orange-plumed salt cedars line its course, taking greedy shares of the brackish water. There is no bridge to Riley, but since the river itself is but a few yards wide, my truck makes a solid crossing.

Riley looks welcoming in the sunshine. The well-kept church, with steeple and cross, and an American flag posted in the churchyard cemetery confirm the feeling. Hispanic farmers who settled here in 1880 named their village—and later their church—Santa Rita. But by the time the post office was granted, the named was changed to Riley, for a local sheep rancher.

The early settlers were farmers and ranchers. But by 1897, mining was the main occupation, with four mines in the area producing gold, silver, and lead. By then some 150 people lived in Riley, which had two stores and a school in session five months a year. A priest came to Riley every four months to say mass at the Santa Rita Catholic Church.

The mines eventually closed, ending that phase of Riley's history. Then the combination of overgrazing and drought lowered the water table such that irrigation was no longer possible. Without mining and agriculture to sustain them, the people drifted away, and finally Riley was abandoned.

Riley today consists of a mission-style stone schoolhouse, under roof but with a rotting floor. Nearby several adobe buildings are melting into the ground, leaving their wooden door frames fallen to the side. The church, however, has been carefully preserved. Riley celebrates a mass there every year on May 22, Santa Rita's feast day. Then the congregation gathers at the covered pavilion next to the church for a picnic. I'm taking my lunch there today out of the cold wind.

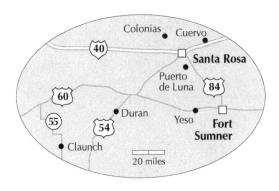

· **6** ·

The Eastern Plains:
Highways and Byways

Colonias · Puerto de Luna · Cuervo · Yeso · Duran · Claunch

Roadside towns are by their very nature history's bystanders. While Santa Fe and Albuquerque made their names as trail and railroad towns, both went on to be known for so much more. Other, less ambitious towns simply faded in place by the roadside, leaving behind but a modest mention of their names.

These are the roadside towns that occupy the upper region tucked between the Rio Grande on the west and the Pecos River on the east. The area's easygoing terrain accommodates great stretches of highway but at the same time fails to give much reason to stop.

Coronado passed north of Puerto de Luna in 1541, but he was just heading for Kansas in his quest for Quivera and its streets of gold. Comancheros came through here in the 1800s, but they were interested only in reaching Texas to trade with the Comanches. When the railroad came through here early in the twentieth century, it created the towns of Yeso, Cuervo, and Duran but used them mainly as water stops.

In 1926, when the federal government created the national highway system, new highways threaded across New Mexico in four directions. The celebrated US Route 66 followed much of Coronado's 1541 course through eastern New Mexico, where it tracked alongside Cuervo but bypassed Puerto de Luna. Yeso already was in place when US Route 60 came through, as was Duran when its road became US 54. Then in 1956 President Dwight D. Eisenhower signed legislation creating interstate highways. The president said the national highway system would "change the face of America." The new Interstate 40 certainly changed the look of Cuervo. As the interstate rolled over Route 66, the four lanes cut Cuervo in half, allowing traffic to zip through town without stopping.

Colonias, one of the earliest towns in the region, continues to exist at its end-of-the-road location, while Claunch, the latecomer, maintains its equally low-profile spot on the map. Today all of the towns remain in place by the roadside, but they are nothing more than observers.

The Claunch Museum (no hours of operation listed), the old bean elevator, and the dance hall—housed in a building constructed of tin, wood, and adobe—stretch down the east side of New Mexico Highway 55.

Colonias

Go 6 miles west of Santa Rosa on I-40. Take exit 267 onto CR 4H and go north 12 miles. The road is paved most of the way.

On the hilltop outside Colonias an American flag flies from a simple white cross. It is a telling introduction to Colonias, a traditional Hispanic village that shows devotion to its religion while giving salute to its nation. It is but a dozen miles from the interstate highway, yet it feels a century removed from the fast lane. Colonias is a poor community where people live in run-down trailers next to abandoned and ruined adobes. Yet they keep up their park and are making a valiant effort to save their church.

Colonias, one of the oldest settlements on the eastern plains, was established in the 1830s as a "colony," meaning a community. The early settlers were farmers who in the fall hunted buffalo along the Pecos River. The river valley opens onto the eastern plains and once was a great hunting ground. Antonio de Espejo, a sixteenth-century explorer, called the Pecos the "river of cows" for the buffalo he found along its stretch.

While the San Jose Church is still the village landmark, it is in a terrible state. Photographs from twenty years ago show the church with its three

Making a valiant effort to rescue the San Jose Church in Colonias, residents of the small 1830s community have tried to stabilize the thick adobe walls and rebuild the historic structure. Work is ongoing, and other than community contributions of time and materials, the donation box at the mission's entrance funds the project.

distinctive towers, one with an ominous crack. Today that tower has fallen away, leaving a gaping hole at the corner of the church. In an attempt to stabilize the church, the gash has been patched with sheets of tin and poorly laid adobes. Now the opposite tower is pulling away. Observing this wasting away is like watching a proud animal downed, wounded beyond saving.

It's a shame, too. If Colonias should lose its church (access to the building already is restricted because it is unsafe), what is to become of the village? The church is a signal, as much as is a cross and a flag, that people still care. Someone, or some group, should drive the dozen miles to Colonias and help save it.

Puerto de Luna

Puerto de Luna is 8.4 miles south of Santa Rosa on NM 91.

Puerto de Luna's lyrical name comes with its own legend. It is said that Coronado camped here on his way to Kansas and, on seeing the moonrise through a gap in the mesa, proclaimed it Puerto de Luna, or "gateway of the moon." The only problem is Coronado's route never came this far south.

Comancheros, however, made a well-worn path through here during the 1800s. Their cart road angled southeast from the Santa Fe Trail to the Pecos River, then followed it past Puerto de Luna to Fort Sumner. From there it crossed the eastern plains to Texas and to their trading partners, the Comanches.

While Josiah Gregg, in *Commerce of the Prairies*, described Comancheros as "composed of the indigent and rude classes of the frontier villages," the traders included a few former U.S. Army officers and some renegade Anglos. At first the Comancheros traded "trinkets and trumperies of all kinds" for buffalo robes, horses, and mules. Later they expanded their line to include guns, knives, and ammunition. In trade, the Comanches offered whole herds of cattle raided from Texas ranches. The U.S. Army put an end to the trading route in 1874 with its campaign against the Comanches on the eastern plains.

By then Puerto de Luna was well established on the Pecos. In the 1860s members of the powerful sheep-ranching Luna family had settled nearby at the mouth of Puerto Creek. When they moved over to the Pecos River in 1862, the settlement became Puerto de Luna, simply "Luna's Gap."

By 1890, it was the county seat and the only town on the eastern plains with a population of more than 500. But in 1902 the railroad came to Santa Rosa, and Puerto de Luna lost its importance and its county seat.

The scenic drive across the Pecos River to the western section of Puerto de Luna rewards visitors with a view of another historic part of the community, where this tiny chapel—surrounded by ancient adobe homes and assorted vehicles—and the old cemetery can be found.

Today the road to Puerto de Luna is simply a detour off the highway. It's a pleasant drive, though, along the tree-lined Pecos River and through fields readied for spring. In town, the old sandstone courthouse stands fenced in the middle of a dirt lot. The Nuestra Senora de Refugio Catholic Church, built in 1882, has been given a bold new face and a tall, shiny steeple. The town is mostly inhabited, with a few old adobe buildings renewed as residences.

Cuervo

Cuervo is 17 miles east of Santa Rosa on I-40.

Cuervo is one of those highway towns that may be more interesting in its decline than when it was alive and kicking on Route 66.

Looking particularly desolate and forlorn on a cloudy winter day, the residential area of Cuervo has been abandoned to the elements. The boxcar house didn't have far to travel, as the town was established to provide service for railroad traffic.

Although Cuervo lay in the path of five centuries' worth of trade and travel routes, it is a twentieth-century town. It was born when the Chicago, Rock Island and Pacific Railroad came through in 1902. The Rock Island's steam locomotives hauled passenger and freight cars from Chicago to California. These big engines needed plenty of water, so smaller towns such as Cuervo served as water stops.

By 1910, Cuervo also had become a trading center for area sheep and cattle ranchers. At its peak, Cuervo, which means "crow" in Spanish, had two of everything—schools, hotels, doctors, and churches. When US Route 66 came through in the 1930s, Cuervo added motels and gas stations to their roadside businesses. By the end of the 1960s, Interstate 40 had followed Route 66, cutting a four-lane swath through town. The interstate not only divided the town in two, it also allowed traffic to cruise on by with nary a glance at Cuervo.

Today the south half of Cuervo shows all the sad evidence of its former

An old truck, a rusting reminder of the days when Route 66 brought prosperity to Cuervo, sits discarded near the deteriorating buildings on Cuervo's south side.

life. Many of the buildings are built of red sandstone blocks, including the Catholic church. While the church is alive and well, the house next door looks recently deserted. The screenless screen door provides a clear view into a room furnished with chairs, a stove, and the discards of its last days as a home. Down the street is a boxcar house, complete with a boxcar addition on back. The skeletal remains of a bus lie in the weedy yard of another deserted house. Erosion has marooned the 1930s sandstone schoolhouse on an island of red dirt. While the building is solid, the inside has been gutted for its wood floors. The school closed in 1958.

The north side of Cuervo is dedicated to the business of car refuel, rescue, and repair. Down a dirt road is another red sandstone church. The sign over the entrance identifies it as Getty's Memorial Baptist Church. Even without the sign, the baptistery at the front of the sanctuary would have identified the denomination. Acoustical ceiling tiles litter the floor. Like the abandoned buildings across the interstate, Getty's church breathed its last not so long ago.

Yeso

Yeso is 20 miles west of Fort Sumner and 35 miles east of Vaughn on US 60. Avoid the dirt road from Puerto de Luna to Yeso.

The map shows a fairly straight shot from Puerto de Luna to Yeso. Although the road is unpaved, I assume the shortcut will save time on a day already well into afternoon. On the way out of town, a guy in a Jeep assures me the road is passable and instructs me to take the right fork at the red sign.

My thirty-mile shortcut consumes two hours and takes me to forked roads leading to more forked roads, down a dead end clotted with cows too lazy to move, and up Salado Creek, dry as a bone, thank God. Then, just as the sun is setting, I pop out onto US 60 not five miles from Yeso.

The sun's last rays light Yeso a fiery red, giving every run-down, pockmarked building the warmth of a Robert Redford movie. In this movie set glow, a two-story hotel at first looks hospitable. In reality, the boarded-up building offers no comfort at all.

Once upon a time, however, Yeso offered plenty of hospitality. It was founded in 1906 on the Santa Fe Railroad route roughly midway between New Mexico's eastern border and Belen on the Rio Grande. The town, which took its name from Yeso Creek, *yeso* meaning gypsum, at first was populated by railroad workers who drank as hard as they worked. Saloons—and their refreshments—proved such a hindrance to worker productivity in

Deteriorating buildings, including the old US Highway 60 hotel, are framed by the shell of a structure adjacent to the tracks at Yeso, a town site selected by the Santa Fe Railroad for its water and location.

Vaughn, the next town west, that the railroad persuaded the courts to shut down the saloons.

It was Yeso's water, though, that allowed it to prosper long after the railroad crews had gone. Its wells provided water not only for the Santa Fe Railroad's steam engines, but also for cattle on nearby ranches. At one time, Yeso was considered for the county seat. Then in the 1930s, when the Santa Fe began converting its steam engines to diesel, water stops at towns like Yeso were no longer necessary. Yeso was reprieved in 1932, however, with the construction of US 60 through town. Eventually, the highway could no longer sustain Yeso.

In the dying light Yeso looks even more like the highway town it once was. A sign painted on the side of the hotel advertises Frontier Museum and Trading Post with Guns and Antiques added in bold lettering. What once was a garage and motel is now just a crumbling stone motel. The east section still has its roof, but the roof on the west side lies crumpled in front. The old post office sits across from the efficiently standard new gray post office. People still live in Yeso, and several other buildings in town are worth seeing—but in the daylight.

Duran

Duran is 16 miles south of Vaughn and 20 miles north of Corona on US 54. The cemetery is off the back road east of town.

In February 1902 the El Paso and Northeastern Railroad completed its "Arrow Route" from El Paso to Santa Rosa, where it linked with the Rock

Blocks of rosy sandstone were used to construct several unique buildings in Duran, including this grand mercantile that apparently offered a little bit of everything to residents in this ranching and railroad community.

Island Railroad. Along the way, the railroad had bought water for their work crews from Blas and Espiridón Durán, brothers who owned wells in the area. There the railroad also built repair shops, including a wooden roundhouse. The settlement that grew up around this division point came to be called Duran after the two brothers. Because Duran was in the middle of a cattle growing region, it also became a supply center for area ranches.

When the railroad moved its shops to Carrizozo, Duran's growth stagnated. The roundhouse was dismantled in 1921. Duran managed to hang on as a ranching center, and when US 54 came through in the 1930s, it benefited from its location on that highway. When north-south Interstate 25 was built, however, it siphoned off traffic from US 54's two-lane route.

Both the railroad and the highway still run through Duran, but there is little reason to stop—except for its remarkable old buildings. West of the railroad tracks is a two-story building of cut sandstone, a faded sign on the front reading Furniture, hardware, grocery, dry goods. The sandstone is unusual in that its buff-colored stones are marbled in white. Several other buildings on the other side of the tracks are built of the same marbled sandstone, including the tall fire station. The range of architectural styles, and the quality of the masonry, also are unusual for such a small community.

Facing the highway, for example, is the 1908 William Hindi Store, with a sign on its wall saying, Tourists Welcome. It is built of cut stone and missing all its windows and doors. On a side street are twin houses built from the same plan, one occupied, the other spookily vacant. One old adobe is losing its whitewashed plaster almost by design. A barn, walls and roof of tin, is a rusted beauty. The redbrick school near the fire station is in near perfect condition and built in a simplified railroad style now back in vogue. The school closed in 1955, and it is now the community center. The San Juan Bautista Catholic Church also appears to be of recent vintage but was built in 1910. Many of the old buildings are still in use, including the fire station, the school, and the church.

Claunch

Claunch is 39 miles south of Mountainair on NM 55.

The southern reach of the Estancia Valley is a sea of short grass and cholla cactus. In a place where a curve in the road counts as a landmark, the sky bears the responsibility for the scenery. And a fine view it is. The sky shows turquoise at the horizon, then deepens to royal blue overhead. While a high wind stirs up the clouds, feathering them at the edges, a buzzard takes a ride on the thermals. Ahead a few buildings sit close to the road like pieces on a board game. Welcome to Claunch.

It is a Saturday morning, and the post office is still open. Benolyn McKibbin, the postmistress, is busy sorting mail just in from Mountainair. The post office has fifty-three boxes, although they're not all rented. McKibbin says that before the post office had boxes, incoming mail was just dumped out on a table. "Everybody would go through it and pick out their own mail," she says.

The post office building also serves as the Claunch Library. It is as comfortable as a parlor, complete with polished hardwood floors, potbellied stove, a couch, and a refrigerator. Books are neatly shelved in bookcases lining two long walls. The books are all donated and are offered for loan or for keeps.

When the town was settled early in the twentieth century, it was called DuBois Flats, after homesteader Frank DuBois, who had sheep and cattle

Thunder from a mountain storm rumbles across the southwest corner of Claunch, where a small, elegant brick house is likely to meet the same fate as the deteriorating schoolhouse to the right.

ranches nearby. Later, homesteading farmers planted pinto beans in the Estancia Valley's fine, fertile soil. From about 1910 through the 1920s, the area was part of a pinto bean boom, leading nearby Mountainair to proclaim itself the "Pinto Bean Capital of the World."

By 1930, DuBois had grown enough to warrant its own post office. Since another town already claimed the DuBois name, the town took the name of L.H. Claunch, after another area rancher. Claunch in the 1930s had a grade school, a library, and a high school built end to end. It also had a store and two churches. The pinto bean elevator was the most prominent building in town.

But about the time Claunch seemed set, the country was well into the Depression. By then the soil that had supported the bean crops was being eroded due to the practice of deep plowing. Droughts in the 1930s and 1940s only added to the erosion problem. Dust storms killed livestock and wiped out entire crops of pinto beans in the Estancia Valley. As the grasslands dried up, ranchers raised fewer cattle or sold out to bigger ranches. While Claunch remained the center of the ranching and farming community, that community grew smaller and smaller. The school closed in 1950, and by the 1960s fewer than ten families lived in Claunch.

Today the schools and their library bear the grim scars of vandalism. However, they are still recognizable, as is a stone store on the corner. The Pinto Bean Elevator features a downed windmill and a sign on the front of the building reading Ye Olde Dance Hall. In addition to the post office and library, Claunch also supports a church and a women's club.

For many years Claunch hosted the Torrance County Singing Convention, a Sunday songfest and reunion of sorts. But eventually that also died out. Today about fifteen people gather at the Claunch Community Church one Sunday a month. "We take turns hunting up a preacher," McKibbin says, "and if that fails, we do the Bible study ourselves."

· 7 ·

Lincoln County:
Billy the Kid Country

Fort Stanton · Lincoln · White Oaks · Jicarilla · Ancho

There are times of high drama in every state's history. For Texas it was the Alamo, for Oklahoma, the Land Rush. But none compares to New Mexico's claim to fame—the legend of Billy the Kid. As much as his place in history has been debated, how, then, to explain the countless books and B movies about his short, scrappy life? Perhaps it's because the saga of Billy the Kid and the Lincoln County War had all the elements of popular drama—a picturesque setting, flawed characters, and shocking violence. Plus a legion of writers to tell the tale.

Lincoln County was created in 1869, and within a decade it had expanded to become the largest county in the United States, an area that included one-fourth of all New Mexico. By then its wide-open spaces had filled with settlers, cattlemen, and fugitives all looking for the same thing—a fresh start. The Civil War and Reconstruction had driven them out of the south, up through Texas, and into Lincoln County, where they arrived hard-edged and handy with a gun.

The government had made things easier for them, first by subduing the Apaches and second by offering the settlers vast tracts of land for practically nothing. Fort Stanton, which lay in the heart of Lincoln County, was charged with keeping an eye on the 400 Mescalero Apaches settled on the White Mountain Reservation. The Indians were issued food and supplies at Fort Stanton. These lucrative supply contracts became the source of fierce competition between rival suppliers, a competition that would escalate into the Lincoln County War.

During this time the government passed the Desert Lands Act, which offered 640-acre tracts of rangeland to settlers for 25 cents an acre. (Unlike homesteaders, they were neither required to live on the land nor to hold citizenship.) At the end of three years, with a final $1-an-acre payment and

Lieutenant and Mrs. Paddock ride along the banks of the Rio Bonito near Fort Stanton in about 1866. The wives and families of officers often lived at frontier forts after the Civil War. Courtesy Museum of New Mexico, #11674.

application for citizenship, the land was theirs. The land offer proved a boon to speculators, who snapped up thousands of acres using bogus names. These big spreads often were stocked with cattle of dubious ownership. Rustling became so commonplace that ranchers hired young guns, "Regulators," to protect their herds.

It was a time when violence outraced law and order and lawmen served solitary, tough duty. Pat Garrett, Lincoln County's sheriff, was a western lawman worthy of study in his own right even had he not been the man who shot Billy the Kid. The six-foot, five-inch Garrett would weave in and out of New Mexico's history until his own violent death in 1908. Garrett was one among a wealth of characters who populated Lincoln's history, a cast that included the doomed Englishman John Tunstall, the feisty Susan McSween, and Billy, the antihero.

Most lived by the Code of the West, rules defined in Texas during the bloody Reconstruction era. Unlike English common law, which called for avoiding confrontation, the Code of the West brooked no compromise. Those who lived by the code never backed down and avenged all wrongs. They could shoot a man over an insult and kill an enemy as long as they warned him first. It was the code of the feud, and it wreaked havoc in Lincoln County.

The violence in Lincoln County spawned its own publishing industry. Everyone, it seemed, was a writer. Billy the Kid wrote pleas to Governor Lew Wallace, who in turn was busy writing *Ben Hur*. Dime novels covered the Kid's exploits, calling him a "young monster," while Pat Garrett sought to tell his side of the story in his money-losing memoir.

In 1879, just as Governor Wallace was reaching a settlement in the Lincoln County War, a wandering prospector chipped off a piece of rock at White Oak Springs and shoved it in his pocket. Gold! As prospectors panned and picked in White Oaks and Jicarilla, the troubles at Lincoln were forgotten. Then at the century's close the railroad built a station at Ancho, where workers took up the respectable trade of brick making. By then Billy the Kid would have been nearly forty.

Fort Stanton

The turnoff to Fort Stanton is 4 miles east of Capitan on US 380. Turn south on NM 214 and go 2.5 miles to the fort. The museum is on the corner of First Street and Lincoln Drive. The cemetery is a mile southeast.

When the army established Fort Stanton in 1855, its role was to protect settlers from the Indians. What the military couldn't know was that the solid old fort would play many roles during its long life.

The fort was named for Captain Henry Whiting Stanton. That January, Mescalero Apaches had ambushed the captain and a dozen soldiers in icy James Canyon in the Sacramento Mountains, killing the captain and two of his men.

Fort Stanton was situated on 1,300 acres of rolling hills through which the Rio Bonito flowed from its source in the White Mountains. Unlike most frontier forts, which were built of adobe, Fort Stanton was "well and substantially built of stone." By May of 1855, 412 men were assigned to the fort.

The Indian campaign that cost Captain Stanton his life was a last gasp for the destitute Mescaleros. They soon began showing up at Fort Stanton looking for food. In exchange for blankets, tobacco, and food, the Indians agreed to give up raiding. "These people," one officer reported, "have all along shown the most friendly disposition, and are doing all they can to prevent the other Mescaleros from depredating."

Fort Stanton also proved a boon for Las Placitas, later called Lincoln. The Hispanic village, some ten miles distant, not only flourished under the

Civilians and soldiers of the Third Infantry gather in front of the quartermaster's building on Fort Stanton in about 1866. During this time Fort Stanton troops were trying to control the countryside against Indian attacks. Courtesy Museum of New Mexico, #11668.

army's protection, it also found the fort a ready market for their produce, hay and beef.

By 1861, however, the Civil War had come to New Mexico and 300 Texans under the command of Lieutenant Colonel John Baylor were marching toward Fort Stanton. As the Confederates advanced, Fort Stanton's commander evacuated the fort, setting fire to the buildings and all the supplies. By the time Baylor arrived, a summer rainstorm had doused the fire, saving the buildings and a good share of the supplies. Soon, however, Apaches drove the Texans back to their stronghold in Mesilla. Free from any control, Indians, as well as bands of Mexican and Anglo outlaws, terrorized the countryside.

The Civil War in New Mexico came to an end the next year and with the Confederates gone, General James H. Carleton and his California Volunteers found themselves in New Mexico with time on their hands. The general decided to use his troops to solve the "Indian problem." He talked Colonel Kit Carson into leading the campaign, ordering him first to reoccupy Fort Stanton. His final instructions to Carson were to kill all the Mescalero men "whenever and wherever you can find them," adding that

A pair of young women reflect both beauty and gravity in one of the earliest
known photographs of the Mescalero Apaches, taken in about 1870.
Courtesy Rio Grande Historical Collections, New Mexico State University
Library, Ms110, 7.3.7. Blazer Family Papers.

if the Indians begged for peace, their chiefs had to surrender to Carleton in Santa Fe.

Carleton's plan worked. In September the defeated Mescaleros, with Chief Cadete as their spokesperson, went to Santa Fe. There Cadete appealed to Carleton, saying:

> You have driven us from our last and best stronghold, and we have no more heart. Do with us as may seem good to you, but do not forget we are men and braves.

There was no negotiation, and by March 1863, 400 Mescalero Apache men, women, and children were confined to the Bosque Redondo Reservation on the Pecos River. The Mescaleros, living on short rations, were miserable in captivity. Quietly they planned their escape. During the night of November 3, 1865, every able-bodied Apache slipped away into the mountains, where the tribe held out for seven more years.

Facing the parade ground and afternoon sun, this grand building is an example of the refined architecture at Fort Stanton, built in 1855 to protect settlers in New Mexico's Sacramento Mountains.

Then, starving and tired of fighting, they began gathering again at Fort Stanton, where they knew they would receive rations. In 1873, the government established the Mescalero Reservation on the eastern slopes of the White and Sacramento mountains, their old homeland. They continued to receive their rations at Fort Stanton, where L.G. Murphy and Emil Fritz, former officers of the California Column, had set themselves up as post traders.

Their original contract called for them to provide food and supplies to some 500 Mescaleros, a total that quickly jumped to 830. Within two years Murphy and Fritz reported issuing supplies to 2,697 Indians. The army, suspecting graft, instituted changes in the system and sent the partners packing. Soon after, Murphy and Fritz were practicing their brand of business from their new store in Lincoln. However, Fort Stanton had not seen the end of their troubles with the Lincoln merchants.

Following the Lincoln County War, action at Fort Stanton involved chasing renegade Indians. Black troops, known as "Buffalo Soldiers," from Fort Stanton helped run Victorio's band into the ground. With the capture of Geronimo marking the end of the Indian Wars, Fort Stanton's role on the frontier was over. By 1893, only fifteen men were stationed at the fort. In 1896 it closed altogether.

Since then, however, the fort's old stone buildings and its hill country setting (now at 24,000 acres) have filled multiple roles. From 1899 to 1953, its facilities were used as the Merchant Marine Hospital to treat seamen for tuberculosis. During World War II part of the fort was used as an internment camp for 410 German sailors who were rescued when their German luxury liner, the *Columbus*, sank in 1939. Apache trackers were enlisted to capture escaped prisoners. A small contingent of Japanese farmers from California also were interned in a separate area on the fort.

In 1953 the state took over the facility, using it as a tuberculosis sanitarium until it closed in 1966. Since then, the fort has served as a hospital for the mentally disabled, a minimum security prison for women, and a halfway house for ex-offenders.

Today Fort Stanton is championed as a "historic and cultural treasure," which, with proper funding, could be turned into a living museum and conference center. Until then, visitors to Fort Stanton are restricted to the area near the museum. However, the fort's oldest buildings and the parade ground can be seen from there.

The Merchant Marine cemetery sits on a hill overlooking the Capitan Mountains. In one corner of the cemetery are the graves of four German sailors from the ocean liner *Columbus*.

The Fort Stanton Museum and the cemetery are open to the public. Donation. (505) 336-7711; *www.FORTSTANTON.com*

Lincoln ▀▀▀▀▀▀▀▀▀▀▀▀

Lincoln is 32 miles east of Carrizozo on US 380 and 7.5 miles from Fort Stanton.

Lincoln was a model nineteenth-century western town. Its one shady street curved east ever so slightly past the courthouse, the store, the hotel, and the church. Territorial-style houses, small but classic, filled in along the way. It was in this picturesque setting that Lincoln also came to define the lawlessness of the West.

The first settlers arrived in 1855, the same year Fort Stanton was founded a few miles upriver. They called it La Placita del Rio Bonito, "village by the pretty river," and did a brisk business selling grain and beef to the army, their sole customer. From the beginning, the thriving community drew an unusual mix of players. By 1860, for example, a quarter of the 276 people who lived there were Anglo, rare for a frontier village. After the Civil War, La Placita would be dominated by former army officers, many of them Irish and German immigrants who had mustered out at Fort Stanton.

Major Lawrence Murphy, who had been an army quartermaster, was ready to cash in on this experience by the time he left the army at Fort Stanton. At once hard drinking and affable, the thirty-five-year-old Murphy and former lieutenant colonel Emil Fritz went into partnership as post traders. They opened a store, a brewery, and a saloon—eighteen rooms in all—on the post proper. While Fritz served as bookkeeper, Murphy went after government contracts. The company soon held a monopoly on the military supply business.

They used their power to gouge the government at every opportunity. The two soon were accused of swindling the Indian agent, charging the soldiers outrageous prices, and operating their store as a place of ill repute.

In 1873 Murphy's shady dealings got him ousted from the fort, but by then he had built a branch store in La Placita, which in 1869 had been designated the county seat and renamed Lincoln. Fritz returned to Germany, where he died the next year, and Murphy took on his former clerk, twenty-five-year-old James J. Dolan, as partner.

Dolan, like Murphy, was an Irish immigrant and former soldier. Murphy sold his building at Fort Stanton for $8,000, then began building a bigger store in Lincoln. The new store housed the mercantile, billiard parlor, and bar on the ground floor and meeting rooms and living quarters on the second floor.

In addition to their store, Murphy and Co. also operated a bank and a restaurant known as Sam Wortley's Mess. The new partnership, however, proved as ruthless as the old one. One pioneer recalled that "Murphy & Co. dominated the country and controlled its people, economy, and politics."

The one man Murphy could not intimidate was John Chisum. He had

Effective protection in a wild town, the *torreon* is an impenetrable adobe tower with tiny gun ports that was used by Lincoln's early residents.

Lincoln's Wortley Hotel, built in 1874, served as Jimmy Dolan's command post during the Five Day Battle in 1878. Among its many owners was Sheriff Pat Garrett, who owned it briefly in the summer of 1881. The hotel burned down in 1936 but was rebuilt in 1960. Courtesy Museum of New Mexico, #110991.

cut his teeth in the cattle business in Texas, where he supplied beef to the Confederate army. After the war Chisum moved his cattle operation to New Mexico, and by 1872, 20,000 of Chisum's cattle were grazing on free rangelands near Roswell. He also set out to sell beef to the army at Fort Stanton, and he didn't want to go through its middleman—Lawrence Murphy.

Meanwhile, in the fall of 1874, Alexander McSween left Kansas, looking for opportunity and for relief for his asthma. Lincoln County seemed to offer both. The thirty-one-year-old McSween, who had once studied to be a Presbyterian minister, arrived in Lincoln with the title of lawyer, a new wife, and not a penny to his name. Susan McSween, ambitious from the start and ruthless to the end, was in bold contrast to her asthmatic, temperate husband. She wore her curls piled high, her dresses fancy, and her face made up. "Mrs. McSween always looked like a big doll," one resident recalled.

McSween turned out to be a good lawyer and nearly always won his cases. His first and most important client was John Chisum. He also was hired to settle the Emil Fritz estate. Then in 1876, while on a trip to Santa Fe, McSween met John Tunstall, a twenty-three-year-old Englishman with family money to invest. In early 1877 the tall, slim Englishman filed claims on 2,300 acres southeast of Lincoln.

Chisum soon allied himself with Alexander McSween and John Tunstall, with some of Chisum's cowboys now working for Tunstall. Tunstall opened a large new store in Lincoln, reserving one room for McSween's law office and another for Chisum's newly organized bank. The Tunstall store was next door to McSween's adobe house and down the street from the Murphy-Dolan store.

About this time Murphy and Dolan were hitting hard times. Low beef prices trimmed profits from their government contracts, and suppliers were demanding payment. Plus Chisum's operation and Tunstall's enterprise meant ruinous competition. In March 1877 Murphy, fading into alcoholism, sold out to Dolan and moved to Santa Fe, where died the next year at age forty-eight.

Dolan, now in charge, demanded that McSween hand over $10,000 in insurance money from the Fritz estate, claiming it belonged to the business. McSween, who conveniently held the money in his own bank account, refused. Dolan charged McSween with embezzlement and had Sheriff William Brady arrest McSween. Dolan then dropped the embezzlement charges in favor of attaching McSween's property to recover the insurance money. Sheriff Brady and a posse barged into McSween's home to inventory his possessions, then went on to Tunstall's store, where, under the assumption that Tunstall and McSween were partners, they seized that property.

By now, the competing factions each had supporters. For Dolan, it was a cadre of Murphy-Dolan thugs, backed by a lineup of questionable officials. For Tunstall and McSween, it was a handful of Hispanic sympathizers in Lincoln, plus a bunch of gunfighters who worked as Tunstall's ranch hands, among them Bill Bonney—Billy the Kid.

Brady, rationalizing that what belonged to Tunstall also belonged to McSween, sent a twenty-four-man posse to Tunstall's ranch to attach his cattle and horses. Fearing violence, Tunstall sent word he would not resist, and on the morning of February 18, 1878, he and four cowboys left the ranch with the horses, heading for Lincoln. Tunstall and two of the men rode with the horses along a narrow trail while the other two, John Middleton and Billy Bonney, rode some 500 yards behind.

In the late afternoon, Tunstall's group crested the canyon, scaring up a flock of wild turkeys beside the trail. While his men rode after the birds, Tunstall stayed with the horses. Then as Middleton and Bonney too topped the hill, Brady's posse came thundering from behind. The two, realizing what was happening, raced toward Tunstall. The posse stormed down the slope, splitting off into the scrub oaks, where they kept Tunstall's cowboys

Bullet holes, created when Billy the Kid shot his way out of the Lincoln County jail, are among the fascinating features of the town's courthouse—formerly the Murphy store and currently a museum operated by the state of New Mexico. The building to the left of the courthouse is the old schoolhouse.

at bay. Tunstall, separated from his men, fired two shots from his English revolver before taking one shot to the chest and a second to the back of the head. His horse took another bullet. The posse laid Tunstall's body on a blanket next to his dead horse. In the winter darkness, Tunstall's men hightailed it to Lincoln.

In Lincoln, Tunstall received a proper Presbyterian funeral, with the minister's wife playing the organ. She later recalled that Billy the Kid and his friends were "armed to the teeth" but added that "Billy's voice was a sweet tenor, and he sang with all his might." McSween busied himself writing his will and arranging for life insurance.

With Tunstall gone, his cowboys looked to McSween for guidance. McSween, though, was lying low at Chisum's ranch. While maintaining their allegiance to McSween, the cowboys, now calling themselves the

Regulators, took care of matters themselves. Dick Brewer, one of the Regulators, was also a "special constable," which gave him the right to issue arrest warrants. Riding under this thin authority, the Regulators went after the men who killed Tunstall. By March, two of Brady's posse were dead. Then on April 1, half a dozen Regulators, including Billy the Kid, ambushed Sheriff Brady and his deputies, including George Peppin, in Lincoln. Two were killed, including Brady.

With Peppin now sheriff, it was Dolan's turn to call the shots. The new sheriff filled his posse with Dolan's men and a collection of murderers and horse thieves. For backup, he enlisted the help of soldiers from Fort Stanton. On June 19 Peppin sent his ruffian posse after McSween. They found McSween and his Regulators near San Patricio, and the two groups set off on a running gun battle. With the arrival of troops from Fort Stanton, the Regulators fled into the mountains.

The chase was called off, however, by Fort Stanton's commanding officer, Colonel Nathan Dudley. Dudley's orders to pull back came by congressional mandate, passed on June 18, prohibiting the military from aiding civil authorities. Dudley, who was both indecisive and contentious, would make the worst use of this ban in the Five Day Battle in the Lincoln County War.

At nightfall on July 14, McSween and his Regulators, now some sixty strong, rode back into Lincoln, ready to make a stand. They divided up between McSween's house and two other locations. The next evening, Peppin's posse rode into town, intent on arresting McSween and his men. The posse, full of bluster and numbering about forty, began shooting at McSween's house. All during the next day, the two factions traded potshots, McSween's men firing from the rooftops and Peppin's from the hillside. The sharpshooters succeeded in killing a horse and a mule. By then most of the residents had fled town, but a few families, including women and children, listened to the gunfire from behind shuttered windows and doors.

With fighting continuing on July 16, Peppin appealed to Colonel Dudley for the loan of a howitzer. Dudley refused the request, sending one of his soldiers into Lincoln to deliver the message. As the trooper rode into town, McSween's men fired on him but missed. The battle continued into the next day, claiming its first casualties. Bystanders in the fray, fearing for their families, sent frantic pleas to Dudley for help.

The next morning, the fifth day of the battle, Dudley marched into Lincoln with a force of four officers, thirty-five soldiers, a twelve-pound mountain howitzer, and a Gatling gun. He announced that he had come only to protect women and children but he also said if fired upon, his troops would return fire. He first surrounded McSween's house with soldiers. Then he aimed the howitzer at Montaño's Store, threatening McSween's men inside. They fled to the protection of the Ellis Store, where McSween's other forces had set up. Dudley then trained his howitzer on the Ellis Store, which sent the whole group—two-thirds of McSween's men—retreating to the hills.

Peppin, seeing the balance change in his favor, sent his posse to McSween's, where they smashed windows, tore down barricades, and prepared to set fire to the house. Susan McSween, fearing for her husband's life, marched down the street to Dudley's camp. She begged Dudley to step in and save her home from burning and pleaded with him to allow her husband to surrender to him rather than to Peppin. Dudley refused on both counts. McSween, in a fury, accused Dudley of condemning her husband to certain death.

The fire burned slowly through the adobe house, then in the afternoon the fire ignited a keg of gunpowder, setting off a small explosion. Susan McSween, her sister, and her sister's five children fled the burning home for shelter nearby. As darkness fell, the blazing house lit up the whole town. Inside, McSween and a handful of his men, including Billy the Kid, planned their escape. Bonney would lead a small group in a dash from one

This lonely church, now used for community gatherings, is one of two in Lincoln—a historic town that looks like a Hollywood Old West set.

side of the house, drawing attention away from McSween and the others, who would escape from another direction. The first group was making good on its escape when light from the flames gave them away. All but one made their dash into the darkness. McSween's group, though, was trapped. Some accounts say McSween offered to surrender but instead shot the approaching deputy. When the firing ended, Alexander McSween lay dead, his body riddled with bullets.

McSween's death did not mean an end to the violence in Lincoln County, but it did create a yearning for law and order. Following the Lincoln County War, James J. Dolan turned his attention to rebuilding his business and his reputation. In 1888 he was elected to the Territorial Senate. Sheriff Peppin, who had been a stone mason in Vermont, went on to build fine houses in Lincoln, including one for Dolan. Susan McSween remarried and moved to White Oaks, where she put her considerable energies to work raising cattle. Colonel Dudley stood accused of several offenses stemming from the events at Lincoln but was eventually cleared of all charges. He was removed from his command at Fort Stanton. Billy the Kid, who played a small role in this drama, would become a western legend.

Today Lincoln appears nearly as it was when Regulators and ruffians rode its streets. Murphy's two-story store became the courthouse. Across the street is the Wortley Hotel. Tunstall's store, as well as those of Montaño and Ellis, still stand. Peppin's house is falling down, but Dolan's is sound and occupied. Where McSween's house once stood is now a weedy lot.

Lincoln's visitor center houses a museum and bookstore. Several of the buildings are open for tours. Fee. (505) 653–4025

White Oaks

From Carrizozo go north on US 54 for 3.1 miles, then turn onto NM 349 for 9 miles to White Oaks.

"I am now in this place, White Oaks, still trying to do business and am very old but supple," Susan McSween wrote a friend in 1928. Following the Lincoln County War, she had invested in a good chunk of property in the fledgling boom town and had moved there permanently in 1903.

White Oaks dates back to 1879, when, as one story goes, John J. Baxter, a refugee from the California gold fields, stopped at a bar in San Antonio, along the Rio Grande. The Mexican bartender told him of a place in the mountains where Spaniards once panned for gold. It was a hard trip, he said,

Miners wearing an interesting array of hats are shown at the Henry Clay Mine near White Oaks. Courtesy Rio Grande Historical Collections, New Mexico State University, RGHC 78-1714. John Stearns Collection.

a hundred miles east, across the *malpais*, the lava "badlands," and into the mountains. Then he drew Baxter a map.

Baxter crossed the tortuous malpais with a mule and a good supply of bourbon. The map led him first to a grove of white-oak trees, then a spring, and finally, voilà! gold. He filed a claim on the mountain but left soon after for the gold fields of Silver City. By then, Baxter's Mountain was crawling with prospectors, including John Wilson and John Winters. This story goes that Wilson went exploring on Baxter's Mountain, taking along his miner's pick. When he stopped for lunch near a massive quartz outcrop, he chipped off a chunk and found it laced with gold. He reported his find to Winters, then promptly sold out to his partner for $40 in gold dust, $2 in silver, a bottle of whiskey, and a broken pistol. The next morning Wilson was gone, some say one step ahead of a Texas lawman.

Winters kept on digging and, four feet down, struck pay dirt. His strike, called the Homestake Mine, eventually played out at $525,000. A few hundred feet from the Homestake Mine, Abe Whiteman set out stakes but, unimpressed with the claim, sold it to William Watson for $1. The Old Abe Mine, named for the hapless Whiteman, yielded $3 million in gold during its lifetime. With the addition of other successful mines like the Little Mack, the Comstock, and the Rip Van Winkle, White Oaks supported a full-scale mining operation. It also helped that White Oaks Springs provided the water needed for the mines and nearby coal deposits provided the fuel for its steam-powered stamp mills.

The town of White Oaks sprang up at the base of Baxter's Mountain in 1879, first as a tent city. On July 17, 1880, the town, now with 800 residents, proudly celebrated the completion of its first real house with several days of nonstop drinking. Even the name of its first newspaper, *The White Oaks Golden Era*, spoke to its unabashed optimism. Its three churches, $10,000 brick schoolhouse, two-story bank building, and two hotels were evidence of its respectability. Not so evident were the "suburbs" of White Oaks. In Hidetown, for example, people lived in shacks and hunters spread out smelly

Massive in comparison to the tin-roofed adobe near it, this gracious red brick mansion—Hoyle's Folly—is named for the man who spent his considerable fortune (and then some) of $42,000 to build the fine home for the girl of his dreams. A nightmare ensued after she rejected his offer of marriage, and he disappeared from White Oaks to avoid repaying an outstanding loan.

buffalo hides to cure. The seamier professions were relegated to Hogtown in buildings dedicated to drinking, whoring, and gambling.

Although Billy the Kid sometimes conducted his rustling business from a local stable, White Oaks was largely spared the violence that shook the rest of Lincoln County. Instead, White Oaks preferred citizens of a different sort. It was home, for example, to lawyer and western writer Emerson Hough, who used White Oaks as the setting for his novel *Heart's Desire*. W.C. McDonald and Harvey B. Fergusson also practiced law in White Oaks. McDonald went on to become New Mexico's first governor following statehood and Fergusson was later a U.S. Congressman.

By 1887, White Oaks had a population of 4,000 and some 200 houses. That year Watson Hoyle, a partner in the Old Abe Mine, completed his grand brick-and-stone mansion. The Victorian masterpiece featured stained glass, hand-carved mantels, and furnishings of the finest style. He built the house to win the hand of a girl back East, but she was not impressed enough even to come to New Mexico. Hoyle lived alone in the house for a while, then disappeared altogether, leaving the bank holding the mortgage on "Hoyle's Folly."

While the mines began to play out in the background, in the late 1880s White Oaks looked to the railroad as its next bonanza. Railroad promoters in El Paso believed the coal deposits in White Oaks would be a cheap source of fuel for their growing city. But their every attempt to build a rail line failed.

When Charles B. Eddy's El Paso and Northeastern Railroad did come through in 1901, it bypassed White Oaks altogether. Instead, Eddy laid track from El Paso past the new towns of Alamogordo and Carrizozo and on through Ancho Canyon. The savvy businessman avoided White Oaks partly because property owners there, thinking Eddy would pay top dollar for a right-of-way, set too high an asking price. Besides, he found the coal fields at White Oaks disappointing and had set his sights on larger deposits up north on John Dawson's land.

White Oaks' winning streak was over. By 1907 only 400 people lived in town, and after a fire shut down the Old Abe Mine in 1930, the population dropped again by half, then bottomed out in the 1950s.

White Oaks today is in something of a revival. Artists have found the old town an agreeable place to practice their craft. The dusty schoolhouse is genuinely charming, as is its tour guide, Robert Leslie. He and his father both attended school there, and his grandfather served on its first school board. Leslie, nearly ninety, wears a watch encrusted with bits of gold he panned on Baxter's Mountain and keeps a gold nugget handy to show visitors.

Nearly every house in White Oaks is occupied these days, including Hoyle's Folly and a pretty Victorian north of the school. The White Oaks

The substantial brick schoolhouse in White Oaks educates the public of today about the town's colorful past in its new role as museum. A white Victorian home, restored and well maintained, emerges from the juniper- and piñon-covered hills north of the gold- and silver-mining community that dates back to 1879.

business district has not fared as well. The Exchange Bank is now just a foundation, its bricks used to build a nearby ranch house. The two-story building that once housed Brown's Store shows signs of a restoration left
unfinished long ago. The ruins of a log Chinese laundry sit back from the
road on the north side of town.

The Cedardale Cemetery at the edge of town is in fine shape. Governor
McDonald is buried there, as is Susan McSween. She died in White Oaks in
1931, at the age of eighty-six. Her grave is covered in lavender and yellow
silk flowers, but her name is misspelled on her new granite tombstone.

*The Schoolhouse Museum is open weekends. Fee. The four-room Miner's
Home and Museum is on White Oaks Ave. Donation.*

Jicarilla

*Jicarilla is 10.6 miles northeast of White Oaks. Take the left fork
leading north from White Oaks onto A041. This U.S. Forest
Service road is dirt but well maintained. The schoolhouse is on
the left about a mile before Jicarilla. Take the left fork just past
the school to the town site.*

The monsoon has filled the sky with fat, towering clouds that promise
more rain. Sunflowers lining the muddy road nod their yellow heads as if
to a passing parade. The road travels through a bowl-shaped valley
whose sloping sides give the mountains their name—Jicarilla, Spanish for
"little cup" or "drinking gourd." Spanish explorers also gave this name to
the Indians they found here. The Jicarilla Apaches, who lived on the
move, carried little woven cups, *jicarillas*, that were both unbreakable and
portable.

The Jicarilla were removed from these southern mountains in the early
1870s and shuttled from one reservation after another until 1887, when
they finally were settled onto their own reservation in northern New
Mexico. By then the Jicarilla Mountains were taken over by another restless breed—gold miners.

Mexican miners had worked the streams as far back as 1850, but with the
Apaches gone and a gold strike in nearby White Oaks in 1879, prospecting
began in earnest. At its peak some 200 people lived in Jicarilla, which had
a general store and a saloon. In 1907 residents built a log schoolhouse, which
on Saturdays doubled as a dance hall.

The prosperity at White Oaks never materialized at Jicarilla. Instead, the
mining camp became a haven of last resort for some 300 families during

Looking like it belongs in an illustration from *Little House in the Big Woods,* this rustic one-room schoolhouse sits by itself on the mountain road that connects White Oaks and Ancho. The log school in Jicarilla, built in 1907, was the site of popular Saturday-night dances in the community, which never quite prospered.

the Depression of the 1930s. Miners then could bring in as much as $7 a week from placer mining and feed their families on wild turkey. Sixty children attended the one-room school.

When the Depression ended, the families left for better times elsewhere, but the Jicarilla they left behind still looks depressing. The remaining original building is the false front store, now boarded up and landscaped in abandoned appliances. The town is seemingly occupied, but on this day, Jicarilla is populated only by two goats, one mule, half a dozen chickens, and a hound dog tied to a tree.

The schoolhouse is rain soaked but appears sturdy under a new tin roof and the protection of the U.S. Forest Service, which has posted a sign reading Enjoy but Do Not Destroy Our American Heritage.

Ancho

To reach Ancho from Carrizozo, go 21 miles north on US 54,
then turn east on NM 482 for 2.5 miles or continue the loop
from White Oaks through Jicarilla to Ancho, which is about
20 miles.

As the El Paso and Northeastern Railroad laid down tracks north from El
Paso in December 1897, it created towns along the way—Alamogordo in
1898 and Carrizozo and Ancho in 1899.

Ancho Valley (*ancho* means "broad" or "wide" in Spanish) was well suited
for railway building. Ancho also was close to both a great deposit of gypsum
and an abundance of good-quality clay. For a time, the little town made the
best of these happy circumstances.

Ancho was at first only a shipping and supply point for local ranchers.
But by 1902 the railroad had built a large station as well as company houses
east of the tracks. That year, the gypsum deposit was discovered and tests
proved local clay to be of brick-making quality. These finds led to the creation of two new industries, the Gypsum Products Company and the
Ancho Brick Plant.

When an earthquake demolished most of San Francisco in 1906, it was
rebuilt using several hundred tons of Ancho plaster. The future looked promising in 1917, when the Phelps Dodge Mining Company bought the brick
plant and enlarged it to sixteen kilns. But the company was never pleased
with the quality of the bricks and closed the plant in 1921.

At one time Ancho had a post office, a couple of stores, and a school with
five teachers and 140 pupils. In 1930, when the old one-room school burned,
Ancho built a new one using Ancho bricks.

But World War II drained away the workforce and homesteaders sold out
to bigger ranchers and moved away. In 1954 the school closed. Then the
next year the new highway bypassed Ancho by three miles. In 1959 even the
railroad canceled its stops at Ancho.

Today a few company houses, small, gray, and abused looking, lie east of
the tracks. On the other side of the tracks is the Ancho school, its rose-tinted
yellow ocher bricks holding up just fine. It is now a church with a congregation of twenty, mostly people from surrounding ranches.

After the depot was abandoned, Jackie Straley Silver bought it and in
1963 had it moved next to her home. Silver, who died in 1972, began
filling the nine rooms with the family's considerable collection of what
she called "old things." She kept the original railroad office intact and
stuffed it with railroad memorabilia. Another room housed the old
Ancho post office (various Straleys served as postmasters for fifty-six

Trains no longer stop at this station in Ancho, but tourists do. Now a museum and gift shop, the depot welcomes twenty-first-century travelers to the community of widely scattered old homes, a sturdy schoolhouse and views of the Sacramento Mountains to the east and the vast Tularosa Basin to the west.

years). The remaining rooms were filled with an incredible array of Ancho and Straley history.

Although the train still goes through Ancho, it hasn't been a railroad town for a long time. Ancho instead is home to a ghost town gem called My House of Old Things.

My House of Old Things Museum is open daily May through Oct. 15. Fee. (505) 648-2456

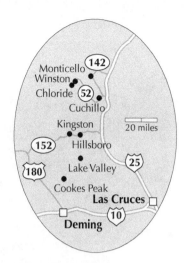

· 8 ·

The Black Range:
When Silver Reigned

Cuchillo · Winston · Chloride · Monticello ·
Hillsboro · Kingston · Lake Valley · Cookes Peak

In 1546, the viceroy of New Spain sent Cristóbal Oñate and his soldiers into Mexico's northern provinces, where Zacatecas Indians were causing trouble. Oñate, who had served under Coronado, quickly restored the peace, then took time out to do a little prospecting. The mines Oñate established in the barren foothills of Zacatecas eventually would yield one-fifth of the world's silver. By the end of the century, Cristóbal's son, Juan de Oñate, would use his father's fortune to finance his colonizing expedition into New Mexico.

Among Oñate's caravan of eighty-three wagons was one carrying a full complement of mining tools and smelting equipment. However, during his fifteen years in New Mexico, he failed to make a single strike. Oñate had chased through northern New Mexico looking for silver when the richest deposits would be found in the ragged mountains to the south and not for another 300 years.

New Mexico during the last twenty years of the nineteenth century was booming. It had recovered from the distractions of the Civil War, and it was a safer place, thanks to the army's efforts at ending the Indian hostilities. The railroad, along with the stage lines and freight companies, had brought transportation—and people—to nearly every corner of the territory. The population had grown from 100,000 in 1880 to 185,000 a decade later.

These were the glory days for silver mining, especially in the mining towns on the eastern flanks of the Black Range. The mines at Kingston, Hillsboro, and Lake Valley alone yielded more than $16 million in silver during this heady period, with Kingston ranking as New Mexico's richest silver producer during the 1800s. The boom was spurred by the passage of the Sherman Silver Purchase Act in 1890. The law required the U.S. Treasury to buy 4.5 million ounces of silver each month (roughly equal to

A welcoming horse, looking for a crisp apple or at least a pat on the head, is the only living creature to be found one recent fall afternoon on Main Street in Winston, the Black Range Mining District's commercial center in better days.

the national production of silver in 1890) and coin it into dollars. Western mining interests favored unlimited, or free, silver coinage for obvious reasons, while farmers saw the increased circulation of money—inflation— as a way to ease the burden of falling farm prices. But when the nation fell into a depression in 1893, proponents of the gold standard blamed free silver as the cause and repealed the act. The short-lived silver boom ended for good with adoption of the gold standard in 1900.

During the twenty-year boom, the silver towns of Chloride, Kingston, Hillsboro, Lake Valley, and Winston led a rollicking, romantic existence. Cuchillo and Monticello led quieter lives nearby, while Cookes Peak, isolated in the brutal mountains to the west, seemed never at peace. These ghost towns, each bearing the distinct features of its past, are New Mexico's best.

The turnoff from I-25 to Cuchillo is 4 miles north of Truth or Consequences at exit 83. Follow NM 181 to the intersection with NM 52, then take NM 52 for 8 miles to Cuchillo.

There was no eureka! moment in the founding of Cuchillo. Instead the village seems to have come into being around 1872, when farmers along Cuchillo Negro Creek began selling their crops at nearby Alamocito (now Monticello) when it was a supply center for the Southern Apaches. The creek itself was named for Chief Cuchillo Negro, or "black knife," a leader of the Warm Springs Apaches. The early settlers were under constant threat of Indian attack until the U.S. Army drove Chief Victorio's band of renegades out of the valley in 1880.

Life is slow paced in Cuchillo, a farming community founded in the early 1870s and named for Cuchillo Negro Creek, which proved to be an unreliable—and sometimes devastating—source of irrigation water.

Occupied during the years when Cuchillo was a hub for mining activities in the mountains to the west, many of the homes and buildings in the town are now inhabited only by memories.

By then Cuchillo was an established Hispanic community whose 233 residents were nearly all farmers. One of the few Anglo residents, Ed Fest, opened a mercantile around 1885 and three years later established the Butterfield Stage Line there. His choice of Cuchillo at first seemed fortunate as it was midway between the mines at Winston and Chloride and the railroad connection at Engle some thirty miles east. For a time he was right.

But when mining fell on hard times in the early 1900s, the stage line was discontinued and Cuchillo lost a third of its population. Agriculture remained Cuchillo's mainstay for another twenty years until repeated flooding also put the farmers out of business.

Cuchillo has hung on over the years, partly because it is only ten miles from the jobs at Truth or Consequences and partly because it is still a roadside town. A summer storm started an electrical fire in Fest's old store on August 28, 2000, burning half the building. The other half survives as a bar that can be lively on occasion. Behind the store are the ruins of a two-story adobe stable. St. Joseph's Church, whitewashed and looking no worse for the wear, was built in 1907 after floods twice destroyed its predecessors. About half the buildings in town are occupied, with the other half in various states of picturesque ruin.

Winston

Winston is 22.5 miles west of Cuchillo on NM 52.

In his 1936 memoir James McKinna wrote, "The beauty of the Black Range cannot be described by man." Allow me.

The road to Winston threads through a succession of conical hills where stands of Spanish broom, live oak, pine, and juniper cluster according to their nature. Where the road angles through a gap in the Sierra Cuchillo, a hundred or so vultures, as thick as black flies, swirl high above unseen carrion. Just as the road levels out, a B-1 bomber barrels down the valley, so low, my truck seems its target. Once it has passed, I'm left with a solitary view of the Black Range, mountains so dense with pines, they look black against the pastel winter sky.

The Black Range is not large by mountain standards, only about 100 miles long and a dozen miles wide. The Continental Divide rides its crest for nearly half the distance and a couple of its peaks reach 10,000 feet. But when prospectors first explored the Black Range in the late 1800s, they concerned themselves not with its beauty, but with what the mountains held in store: gold, silver, lead, and copper.

Surrounded by the truly enchanted landscape of the town first known as Fairview, Winston's schoolhouse is down a long dirt road east of the central part of the mining community.

One of those prospectors discovered silver in Chloride Canyon in 1879. His discovery set in motion the creation of two mining towns in 1881, Chloride and its neighbor up the road, Fairview. Named for its bucolic setting, Fairview was the commercial center for the Black Range Mining District. Its businesses included a mercantile, grocery store, meat market, and hotel, plus a stage that ran daily to the railroad station at Engle. As for the finer things, Fairview had its church, a school, and a literary club. Although it reported a population of 500 at its peak in 1883, its population hovered around 100 from then on.

Frank Winston had been a miner before he came to Fairview in 1882 to open a general store. His new profession suited him well, as did his positions as postmaster and owner of the Fairview Cattle Company and the Fairview Garage. When the bottom dropped out of the silver market and the mines began to close, Winston continued to give credit at his store, knowing it might never be paid. He died in 1929, and the next year Fairview was renamed Winston in honor of his generous spirit.

Today Winston is a two-street town that looks exhausted from more than a century of hanging on. Here mobile homes and run-down historical houses sit side by side in yards framed by tall weeds, brown and gone to seed. At one end of the old Main Street, a few false-front buildings decay at their leisure. One old adobe, which may have been the Fairview Garage, seems spared by its unique features—a mansard roof and corner posts—all of rusted pressed tin. On the road east of the garage, the 1886 schoolhouse, under roof and in repair, sits in a field of amber grass.

On Winston's west road the pretty Victorian built by mining engineer Tom Scales still wears its lacy trim, painted a soft green but peeling just the same. Frank Winston's house up the street is recognizable by its tall peaked roof and its single bay window.

Winston, like many near ghost towns, occupies that narrow space between ruin and revival. But unlike them, Winston also dwells in a place beautiful beyond description.

This inhabited adobe building, perhaps the old Fairview Garage, is far from ordinary, with its decorative pressed tin trim and primitive tractor displayed in front.

Chloride

Go south on the road that skirts Winston on the west, then follow the gravel road for 3 miles to Chloride.

A town that takes the trouble to pave its mile-long street is no ordinary ghost town. Chloride's civic pride seems as strong today, with its population of fifteen, as it was during its heyday, when 500 people lived there.

A mule skinner and inveterate prospector named Harry Pye brought first notice to the shallow canyon where Chloride now stands. While on a supply run for the army in 1879, Pye bedded down his mules where a brushy creek threaded between the canyon walls. Victorio's murderous renegades were on the loose that year, so the canyon's dark mouth hid Pye from sight.

As he broke camp the next day, he picked up a rock fallen from a nearby outcrop and recognized it as silver chloride, the pearly gray crust that forms when silver ore is exposed to the air. He chipped a sample from the outcrop, then went about his business with the army. Later he returned with a group of friends and staked claims on the Pye Lode. He set up camp again, only this time he chose a spot where the canyon yawned onto the open valley. Apaches ambushed and killed Pye there a few months later.

Chief Nana and his Apaches attacked a group of eighteen miners at nearly the same spot in January 1881, killing two of the men. Undaunted, the men bought more guns and ammunition and were back prospecting by March. In April, sixty miners, including James Dalglish, met at Dalglish's new store to lay plans for a town. Town lots, each twenty-five feet by 100 feet, were sold by lottery to the miners. The founders, in an effort to attract more women to town, offered a free lot to the first woman to make Chloride her home.

Within six months, Chloride had twenty-four commercial buildings, including eight saloons and a fruit and confectionary store. The *New Mexican Mining News* reported construction of "a large stone building to be used as a bank" as well as news of a railroad "planned from Socorro to Chloride." The shade trees planted along both sides of Chloride's one street so impressed the editor that he boasted "Chloride is indeed putting on metropolitan airs." Saloon taxes helped support the Chloride school, which in 1884 counted twenty-one students. However, the town never had a church.

Regardless of its wishful image as a metropolis, Chloride in the 1880s was still a dangerous place. Parents kept their children from attending school for fear Apaches would kidnap them. Lookouts were posted to guard the horses from Indian raids. Mail delivery was often delayed because riders were afraid to attempt the trip from Cuchillo to Chloride during Indian

This 1890-95-era photo shows miners at the head frame of the "U.S. Treasury Mine" at Chloride. The head frame's pulley is attached to a platform that transports both men and mining buckets in and out of the vertical mine shaft. Courtesy Museum of New Mexico, #12634. Henry A. Schmidt photograph.

Sometime around 1890-95, Henry A. Schmidt took this panoramic view of Chloride looking southeast. The live oak in the center of town is still alive midway on the main street. Schmidt's priceless collection of 1,500 photographs, many of them on glass plates, documented life in mining towns throughout the Black Range. Courtesy Museum of New Mexico, #13782. Henry A. Schmidt photograph.

scares. The Chloride Militia was organized in 1881 to protect the miners and settlers from Indian attack. As part of the New Mexico Militia, the Chloride unit, under the command of Captain James B. Blain, furnished men, forty Sharpes rifles, and ammunition for its own defense. Blain's adobe house served as the headquarters, and sometimes the barracks, for Chloride's militia.

One member of the militia was a German immigrant named Henry A. Schmidt, who worked as an assayer, chemist, and metallurgist. Schmidt also operated a photography studio in Chloride. His assay skills eventually gave way to a talent for photography.

Schmidt's photographs captured a way of life in the Black Range that was over by the turn of the century. When the government chose gold as the monetary standard, the demand for silver fell and Chloride's fortunes declined in turn.

Remarkably, Chloride today looks much like it did in one of Schmidt's photographs taken a century ago. One reason for its preservation is that since Chloride was owned by individuals, not a mining company, its properties passed on to the descendants of Chloride's pioneers. Also, because a few people continued to live in town, their presence served to deter vandals. But the main reason Chloride looks so good for its age dates to 1976, when a couple took a wrong turn at Winston and ended up in Chloride.

Don and Dona Edmund, who had lived in thirteen states, were looking for a place to retire when they stumbled onto Chloride. They bought an old house in town and at first planned to burn it down and build a new one. "Instead," Don Edmund says, "the more we learned about the history here, the more we wanted to restore the house." In the twenty years since, the Edmunds have bought thirteen buildings in town. Seven have been renovated and five of those are on the State Historic Register.

Apache raids kept early residents edgy in Chloride, subdivided into tidy lots of twenty-five feet by 100 feet in 1881. The village remains the site of distinctive false fronts and adobe homes.

This 1913 photograph shows the Silver Monument Mine crew and their families in front of a Chloride building that once housed the office of Judge E. F. Holmes. Courtesy Rio Grande Historical Collections, New Mexico State University Library, Ms03330027. Henry A. Schmidt photograph.

Their greatest find has been James Dalglish's old store, which closed in 1923. When the Edmunds bought it in 1989, they found the store just as it had been left, complete with cash register, merchandise, and safe—plus "about a thousand bats." After cleaning out the bat droppings, the couple renovated the building and reopened it as a museum.

Some twenty-one buildings in town are recognizable from Schmidt's early photographs, including the never completed stone bank, Captain Blain's house, and the false front building that housed Judge E.F. Holmes's office. Smack in the middle of the street stands Chloride's 200-year-old live oak tree.

Just south of the tree, a bumpy dirt road climbs the steep hill to the Greenwood Cemetery, where the view takes in the Cuchillo Mountains to the east. Frank Winston is buried there, as is Henry Schmidt's son Raymond. Raymond lived in Chloride most of his life and died in 1996 at the age of ninety-eight, the last of Chloride's pioneer sons.

The Pioneer Store Museum is open whenever the Edmunds are in town. Free.

Monticello

*Monticello is northwest of Cuchillo. Take NM 142 for 13.2 miles
north from the junction of NM 142 and NM 52, a few miles east
of Cuchillo. To reach the cemetery take the road off the southwest
corner of the plaza. Go past two cattle guards and up the hill,
staying to the right, to the barbed wire gate. Close the gate
behind you.*

The road to Monticello follows the Alamosa River, a great swath of dry riverbed
filled with rocks washed from the hillsides and pummeled into gravel. The road
eases down and across the dry bed at Placitas, a tiny village on the north bank.
A little farther on, the road slips into Monticello at its plaza, where huge
cottonwood trees throw long blue shadows across the deserted square.

A fortress in times of Apache attacks, the Monticello plaza is peaceful these days—as is the
entire community, founded as Cañada Alamosa in 1856.

The tight little plaza is lined on three sides with adobe buildings, uniformly brown and all wearing the same lead gray corrugated roofs. San Ignacio Catholic Church, a soft eggshell color, takes its proper place on the north side of the plaza. The stately church dates to 1867.

If Monticello bears the look of a village fortress, it is with good reason. It was founded in 1856 in the middle of Apache territory and well before the army provided adequate protection from Indian raids. Their plaza was, in fact, their fortress. The farming and ranching community originally was called Cañada Alamosa for its cottonwood-lined canyon. The village briefly was headquarters for the Southern Apache Agency and as such was home to 500 Apaches. In 1874 the Indians were moved onto the Ojo Caliente Apache Reservation in the Monticello Box Canyon.

Cañada Alamosa was forced to trade in its lyrical name in 1892 when Alphonse Bourguet applied for a post office. Post office policy at that time required all post office locations to have simple, one-word designations. Alphonse and his brother Aristide were French immigrants who had settled in Cañada Alamosa in 1874. It is said that Aristide, in submitting the name Monticello, chose it because Alphonse had once been the postmaster at Monticello, New York.

Monticello still has a post office and one or two people named Bourguet. Its plaza is home to some nine residents, with the valley counting a population of about 100. Just off the plaza's southwest corner is the hull of the Monticello Public School, built by the WPA in 1935.

The cemetery sits on a bluff high above the river with a view unbroken north to south. Where the river has shouldered aside the hills, open fields are being readied for spring. As the sun lowers beneath the heavy clouds, it casts its last light on the white headstones, then leaves the valley to its winter blues.

Hillsboro

Hillsboro is 16 miles west of I-25 on NM 152.

When Sarah Jane Creech settled in Hillsboro in 1886, she had been in America only a short while and bore the manner and dress of a refined Englishwoman. She was a striking beauty—black haired, blue-eyed—whose silks and satins showed off her fashionably tiny waist. Sadie, as they called her, was a sharp, seasoned businesswoman of twenty-one who had come to Hillsboro to open a whorehouse.

She already had been running a house in Kingston, the raucous mining town up the road. But she soon saw the opportunity to expand into

The miner at left is using a sluice box to wash gold from gravel along a creek near Hillsboro. Placer mining appealed to the lone miner as it required only a wooden sluice box, access to a "place" near a stream, and a good measure of luck. Courtesy Museum of New Mexico, #148169.

Hillsboro. It had been named the Sierra County seat in 1884, and the place was thick with miners, soldiers, businessmen, and lawyers—all potential customers.

Sadie opened the Ocean Grove Hotel at the east end of Hillsboro's main street. About that time she married J. W. Orchard, and the two started a stage line. The line consisted of two Concord stages, a freight wagon, a stable of sixty-five horses, and two drivers (not including Sadie, who sometimes pitched in). The stage left Kingston at 2:00 A.M., making stops at Hillsboro and Lake Valley before meeting the 6:00 A.M. train at Nutt. Sadie didn't see the need to branch out to these towns as the stage also delivered customers, a dozen at a time, right to her doorstep. Her hotel served fine food and imported wines and her girls dressed in the latest fashions. Hillsboro was the belle of the Black Range.

Hillsboro's Sierra County Courthouse and Union Church to its right were built in 1892. The courthouse was sold in 1939 for $440, mainly for its bricks, which were used in constructing the new courthouse in Hot Springs. The church is still in use. Courtesy Museum of New Mexico, #76553. George T. Miller photograph.

Hillsboro traced its beginnings to April 1877, when a couple of prospectors discovered gold along Percha Creek. Their discovery set off a mini–gold rush and Hillsboro was born four months later. By the end of the year the gulches around Hillsboro were teeming with prospectors looking for placer gold. Eventually $6 million in silver and gold were taken from the mines around Hillsboro.

Sadie's enterprise notwithstanding, Hillsboro had become a respectable town by the mid-1880s. One reason is that Hillsboro, unlike those mining towns that were decidedly adult and male, attracted families with children. For example, of the 376 people who lived there in 1885, a third were children. Hillsboro's houses were built in styles ranging from simplified Victorians to long, low adobes. One owner took advantage of the nearby

Punishment was not pleasant for prisoners in the Hillsboro jail, with its cramped cells divided by heavy barred doors. Small trees, shrubs, and rattlesnakes have taken up residence in the old rock rooms since the structure lost its roof.

smelter and constructed his house using blocks of slag, the black iridescent by-product of smelted gold. The town had a post office by 1879, a brick schoolhouse by 1882, a newspaper, two churches, and in 1892 a two-story $17,000 brick courthouse.

By the end of the 1890s Hillsboro's fortunes were on the wane. Its politicians were divided by the national debate over the gold standard. Some sided with the "silverites," who favored free silver, while others sided with the "gold bugs," who favored the gold standard. The Black Range newspaper reported, "Politics are hot here, as shown by the little spats that have occurred in our streets. . . . No blood was spilt but lots of wind was wasted." By the time the debate was over, Hillsboro's mines were nearly played out anyway. One by one the big mines shut down—the Snake in 1893 and the Opportunity and the Bonanza in 1894.

In the spring of 1899 Hillsboro saw its last boom. Tents were thrown up at either end of town to house the throngs, bartenders went to three shifts, and Sadie Orchard readied her hotel for prominent guests. Western Union set up a telegraph line from the railroad to Hillsboro, manning it with two operators. Reporters from throughout New Mexico as well as from the *Los Angeles Times* and the Associated Press were in town. However, the excitement was generated not by gold, but by a murder case.

On February 1, 1896, Albert J. Fountain and his eight-year-old son were believed murdered in the desert east of Las Cruces. Fountain, a prominent lawyer and political leader in the Mesilla Valley, had been vigorously prosecuting cattle thieves in the Tularosa Basin when he and his son disappeared. Pat Garrett, the sheriff who killed Billy the Kid, was hired to track down the killers, thought to be Oliver Lee, Bill McNew, and Jim Gilliland. The three were tough cowboys from Texas who ran cattle of questionable ownership on Lee's Tularosa ranch. Garrett got McNew first. After eight months in hiding, Lee and Gilliland finally surrendered to their friend and temporary deputy Eugene Manlove Rhodes. Lee and Gilliland were brought to trial in Hillsboro on a change of venue.

By then the case had turned into a celebrated political feud between Democrats, who promoted the cowboys' innocence, and Republicans, who were just as sure of their guilt. Albert Bacon Fall, an ambitious Democrat, represented the cowboys, while Thomas Catron, a Republican and leader of the land-grabbing Santa Fe Ring, spoke for the prosecution. Both lawyers, as well as the trial judge, stayed at Sadie's hotel. Lee and Gilliland found accommodations at the new jail under the guard of Deputy Rhodes.

Eighteen days and seventy-five witnesses later, the lawyers finished their closing statements. It was 10:30 at night, and the jury headed for bed. An hour later they were called back at the insistence of Fall, who demanded a verdict. Their deliberations took eight minutes. Not guilty. The case was

Hillsboro's fine brick 1892 courthouse, the location of the famous Fountain murder trial, crumbles high on a hill overlooking the town, which is still very much alive.

never solved. Lee went back to ranching and on to the state legislature, while Rhodes drew on his New Mexico adventures to write a dozen or more novels. Garrett was murdered outside of Las Cruces in 1908, and Fall and Catron both became the first U.S. Senators from New Mexico when it became a state in 1912.

That year, Hillsboro's population was holding at about 500. But the town never recovered from the flood of 1914. On June 10, floodwaters from Percha Creek swept down the main street, destroying nearly every adobe building in their path and drowning Thomas Murphy, the county's first sheriff. In 1938 Hillsboro lost the county seat to Hot Springs, now Truth or Consequences, despite Sadie Orchard's legal efforts to block the move. She died in 1943.

Today some 200 people live in Hillsboro, which has become a shady retreat for retirees, writers, and artists. Lovely nineteenth-century homes line its two streets. All that remains of the courthouse is an arched wall. Both churches are in fine shape and fill on certain Sundays. The brick schoolhouse is a private residence, and the old high school is a community center and library. You still can eat and drink in Hillsboro, but not at Sadie Orchard's old hotel. It is now the Black Range Museum.

The Black Range Museum is open Thursday through Sunday. Fee. (505) 895-5233; www.nmculture.org

Kingston

Kingston is 8.5 miles west of Hillsboro on NM 152 where the road angles on the right from the highway. The cemetery is 0.5 mile north of Kingston on NM 152. Park at the second entrance on the right.

From the looks of Kingston today, it is difficult to imagine that 7,000 people once lived here. Most likely, that total counted a few thousand miners camped in the outlying gulches. They swelled the population every time

The Percha Bank is the second building from the front in this view of Kingston in about 1885. Courtesy Museum of New Mexico, #99819. J. C. Burge photograph.

An inviting retreat in the Gila National Forest, the Black Range Lodge contains sections that are built from the stone walls and beamed ceilings of Pretty Sam's Casino and the Monarch Saloon—popular establishments in this silver town that once accommodated a population of 7,000.

they came into town to patronize, for example, its fourteen grocery stores, three hotels, and twenty-two saloons, one of which offered eighty-one brands of whiskey alone.

A couple of prospectors discovered silver in the hills around Kingston in 1880 and established the Iron King and Empire mines. But the Black Range still was Apache country, and Victorio and his renegades soon drove them away. Then in 1882 Jack Sheddon stopped for a boozy nap near there on his way to the mines at Chloride. When he awoke, he was sobered to discover that the boulder where he had rested bore a telltale metallic look. He chipped off a piece and found it rich in silver ore. Sheddon's strike, called the Solitaire, led to the founding of Kingston ten days later on August 16. The new town was named for the Iron King Mine.

Town lots at first went for $25 each, but as miners hit pay dirt, the price jumped to $5,000 in a single month. Soon Kingston's population reached 1,800. A year later it went to 5,000, before topping out at 7,000 in 1884. The twenty-seven silver mines operating at Kingston eventually yielded $6,250,000 in silver, making it the richest silver producer in New Mexico during the nineteenth century.

Kingston's boisterous early years produced many an exciting tale. James McKenna, an adventurer who arrived in Kingston near the beginning, told those stories best in his *Black Range Tales*. One involved Kingston's first Christmas party.

Pretty Sam had worked hard to complete his dance hall, called the Casino, in time for its grand opening on Christmas Eve, 1882. He had invited bigwigs from Kingston, Hillsboro, Silver City, and Lake Valley, offering them free food and drink and dancing to an orchestra from El Paso.

The huge dance hall was built with its entrance at street level. At its back, though, the land plunged thirty feet to the creek below. Pretty Sam had shored up the rear of the building with a trestle, intending to build a bridge from the double doors at the back to the other side of the creek. But since he hadn't finished the bridge, he simply bolted the doors shut.

The crowd, which included at least five colonels in uniform, was in fine dress. McKenna reported that "Ed Doheny and Neil Boyle were two of the dudes who appeared in dress suits rented from El Paso," while the "girls" were in "high feather." Colonel Parker and Big Annie led the grand march. The old colonel, who weighed some 275 pounds, was squeezed into his old West Point uniform, while Big Annie, a "corn-fed" madam from Missouri, was "dressed to kill."

The dance hall was roaring at midnight when a down-on-his-luck gambler showed up with a rifle looking for his girlfriend, a "Denver dame" who had gone to the dance without him. He started shooting, then everyone started shooting, and the crowd rushed for the doors—including those at the back. Big Annie went out first, screaming as she landed in the dry creek bed below. Others followed, piling in a heap on top of Big Annie.

The next afternoon, with Big Annie recuperating from her fall and the gambler under arrest, Kingston celebrated Christmas. The Catholics gathered at Mrs. O'Boyle's cabin for food, hymns, and prayers, while the Protestants met at Pretty Sam's Casino for a service led by an ex-Episcopal priest known as The Duck.

The well-dressed Doheny later would become friends with another Kingston miner—Albert Fall. Doheny went on to make millions in oil, while Fall rose to become the secretary of the interior. Their involvement in the Teapot Dome oil scandal would lead to charges of bribery, for which Fall would go to prison.

By the end of the century, Kingston's mines were exhausted. Flood and fire then did their part to destroy the town. Only three buildings are left to show for Kingston's short, rowdy life as a boomtown—the Percha Bank, an

The old assay office, which was crowded with miners in the past, has been converted into a home that peacefully soaks up the winter sun in Kingston.

assay office, and what's left of the Victorio Hotel. Instead today's Kingston is a tame mountain town of retirees, innkeepers, and straw-bale builders.

The 1882 cemetery may be Kingston's best legacy. The early graves were laid out not in rows, but instead were grouped where dynamite could blast through the rocky soil. Today these graves lie clustered at the end of meandering paths under the shelter of pretty pines.

Lake Valley

Lake Valley is 18 miles south of Hillsboro on NM 27. The cemetery is south across the highway. The road travels through open range, so be alert to livestock and wildlife on the road.

Lake Valley, home of the rich Bridal Chamber Mine, which produced more than $3 million of ore, sprawls beneath the ghost town's cemetery. Many of its buildings were destroyed during a fire in 1895.

Eleven men and a baby pose in front of the cavernous Bridal Chamber Mine in about 1890.
The mine still belongs to an heir of the Sierra Grande Mining company, its original owner.
Courtesy Museum of New Mexico, #56219. Henry A. Schmidt photograph.

After a stop for bumble berry pie in Hillsboro, we take the open road to
Lake Valley. I'm in the company of a sixth grader, a city boy on his way to
visit his first true ghost town. He's brought along a notebook in which he
has carefully noted the speed limit and the presence of a coyote on the road.
Eventually, his notes will run to twelve pages.

We've left the pine-darkened foothills behind and travel through grazing
lands thick with gramma grass. The road dips again and again where creeks
cross on their way to the Rio Grande. Ahead are the barren hills of volcanoes spent aeons ago, a view that suffers from poor winter lighting and a sky
uniformly gray.

Lake Valley, tinted the same matte gray, looks foreboding. A cold wind
rattles the screen door of a house where tattered curtains cover its windows.
On the porch next door, two big armchairs, bleached white by the sun and
losing their stuffing, sit side by side. At their knees is a small white tricycle,
surely a grandchild's toy. The note taker thinks he hears someone inside but
later attributes the "creaking" noise to his imagination. It is spooky, all right.

Lake Valley got its start the usual way. In the summer of 1878 a lone Chinaman taking a shortcut to Silver City comes across an outcropping he thinks is iron. He breaks off a piece, then, before he reaches Silver City, wanders into Georgetown, where miners there recognize the ore as pure silver. Trouble is, the Chinaman forgets where he found it. So two partners, George Lufkin and Chris Watson, go looking for the spot and they find it.

They load a wagon with a thousand pounds of ore and take it to Silver City, where they stop at the Red Onion Saloon to show off their find. A savvy miner named John A. Miller buys the whole load for $1,500. He has the ore assayed and two days later puts up $25,000 in partnership to develop the mine. In 1881, the three sell out to a syndicate headed by George Daly. Miller clears $100,000, with Lufkin and Watson each getting $25,000. Lufkin turns to selling real estate in Daly's mining camp, which soon becomes known as Lake Valley.

It is now 1882, and blacksmith John Levitt leases a claim from the Sierra Grande Mining Company, which controls the Lake Valley mines. Levitt chooses a hole that Lufkin and Watson had started earlier. Forty feet down he punches into a cavern lined in pure silver. Levitt, apparently not realizing what he has found, sells out to the company for a few thousand dollars. Company officials name their windfall the Bridal Chamber Mine.

Teams of oxen haul wagons from the mines down Lake Valley's main street past a clothing store, saloon, and assay office. Courtesy Museum of New Mexico, #100726. Lovell photograph.

Except for the fluorescent light fixtures, the school at Lake Valley looks as if the students from the 1880s just stepped out for recess in this town acquired by the Bureau of Land Management.

The mine's "chamber" was a hollow twenty-six feet across and twelve feet high. Its silver coating was so pure that the flame of one candle could melt silver drippings from the ceiling. Since the cavern was near the surface, the company simply knocked out the side of the hill and ran a spur track straight into the opening. Mining consisted of sawing chunks of silver from the walls and putting them in the railcars at hand. Between 1882 and 1893, the Bridal Chamber Mine yielded more than $3 million in silver.

In 1884 the railroad came to Lake Valley, which by then contained the requisite saloons and outlaws common to mining towns. It laid claim to a peak population of 1,000.

In 1893, when President Cleveland selected gold as the monetary standard, it ended the silver boom in the West. But by then, the Bridal Chamber Mine already was spent. Two years later, most of the buildings on Lake Valley's main street burned to the ground. The Santa Fe Railroad took up its tracks in 1934 and the post office closed in 1954. Lake Valley's last residents, Pedro and Savina Martinez, moved away in 1994. That year, Lake Valley was deeded to the Bureau of Land Management. Since then the BLM has restored the 1904 schoolhouse and has nearly finished restoring the St. Columba Episcopal Church. Several other buildings remain in a state of decline fitting for a ghost town.

It is bitter cold by the time the boy and I make it over to the schoolhouse, where we are greeted by Shelby Caddell, an older man bundled against the cold. He and his wife live in town as caretakers. Since we are the day's only visitors, the stove has not been lit and the school's one big room feels like a walk-in freezer. Caddell shows us around the school, half of which is a furnished classroom and half of which is a museum of sorts.

Back outside, our cheerful host leaves us with a pamphlet about Lake Valley. The boy sits on the stone cold steps of the schoolhouse, hunched over his notebook, his fleece jacket a bloodred spot of color in an otherwise lifeless town.

The Lake Valley School is open daily. Donation.

Cookes Peak

From Deming, take NM 26 northeast 15 miles to the stock pens at Florida. Turn north on CR A019 and go for 10 miles on this dirt road to some stone foundations. A few yards north, take the very rough road west a short distance to the locked gate. You can view the Hadley ruins from here. To reach Cookes Spring and Fort Cummings, backtrack to the A019 turnoff at Florida. Then go back north 1 mile and just past the cattle guard turn west and go 4.5 miles to the fort. Cookes Spring is a quarter mile southwest of the fort.

When Cookes Peak shoved its granite snout through the top of the mountain 27 million years ago, its volcanic act sent boulders crashing down the 8,400-foot mountain. Today those broken boulders form a rocky ring around its base.

Apaches called the peak Standing Mountain, but Americans who forged the wagon road through here in 1846 renamed it Cookes Peak for their trail-blazing commander, Lieutenant Colonel Philip St. George Cooke. Cooke, a six-foot, four-inch West Point graduate, had been chosen to lead a group of Mormon volunteers to California.

Under a unique arrangement between President James Polk and the Mormon leader Brigham Young, a battalion of 500 Mormon men agreed to

Surrounded by a tangle of vegetation, the spring house that collected and diverted water to the railroad at Florida is the only remaining structure at Cookes Spring. The spare ruins of Fort Cummings are nearby.

serve in the U.S. Army for one year. The Mormons had been persecuted at their settlement in Nauvoo, Illinois, and were looking for a promised land farther west, possibly California. But they lacked the funds for such an expedition. Meanwhile, the United States in its war with Mexico was determined to occupy the southwest from Texas to California.

As such, the army needed a viable overland wagon route for moving troops and supplies through the region. So, it was agreed that the Mormon Battalion would receive army pay, rations, and supplies for the trip to California, and in return, they would carve the army its wagon road across the Southwest.

Cooke took command of the battalion at Santa Fe in mid-October. There he culled the men unfit to march, plus most of the women and children, including twenty wives who had been paid as laundresses for the trip. By the time the battalion left the Rio Grande near present-day Hatch, Cooke's command included 339 men, four women, fifteen wagons, and a herd of cattle and sheep. Their westward route took them past a towering peak, where in a nearby ravine some men found a deserted vineyard with plump grapes hanging from the vines. The next day, November 16, they made camp at a "marshy water hole"—Cookes Spring—where several old Indian trails converged. Most of Cooke's wagon road to California, in fact, followed the earlier trails of Indians, Spaniards, and Mexicans.

The Mormon Battalion reached San Diego in January 1847. Cooke left to join the war in Mexico, and many of the Mormons stayed in California to work on farms and ranches. Six from the former battalion were helping build Sutter's sawmill when gold was discovered there in 1848. By then Brigham Young had sent another group of Mormons off to the salt lakes in Utah.

Forty-niners headed for California's gold fields took Cooke's route, as did the Butterfield Stage, which opened a "swing" station at Cookes Spring,

An unnatural landscape, created from tailings that have eroded into soft hills, is a sign of mining—and possibly a ghost town site. Such is the case of Hadley, one of the tiny communities that sprang up around Cookes Peak in Luna County.

where the stage line changed horses. The army established Fort Cummings in 1863 at Cookes Spring to protect the thousands of travelers who passed through the Indian country on their way west.

It wasn't until about 1877, however, that anyone considered the peak for its mineral potential. Edward Orr, who had a ranch about nine miles from Cookes Peak, and Lon Irington were prospecting nearby when they located the silver-rich Blackhawk Mine. The vein, some fifteen feet from the surface, was ten feet wide. The two were able to dig out five to six tons a day but had no efficient way to ship it out. Besides, Apaches were warring and few miners wanted to risk their wrath.

By 1881, however, the Indians had been subdued and the railroad had built a junction some fifteen miles from the mines. When George L. Brooks graded a wagon road down Hadley Draw to the junction, the mines stepped up production. (Hadley Draw was named for Walter C. Hadley, a mining engineer and the son of Hiram Hadley, a founder and the first president of New Mexico State University.) Brooks hauled out the first load of ore and within a short time had shipped out 2,700 tons.

Cookes Peak miners scattered among three camps, Jose on the peak's west slope and Cooks (which dropped the *e* from its name) and Hadley on the east slope. By 1890 the Cookes Peak Mining District was one of the most prolific lead-producing regions in the Southwest. The district's 150 miners worked ten-hour shifts, with Anglo miners earning $3 a day and Mexican miners half that. Throughout 1891, the mines produced an average 800 tons a month with a ton of ore averaging 30 percent lead and containing 80 ounces of silver.

In the process of mining, however, miners were inhaling toxic lead dust. What didn't kill them outright caused terrible physical and mental side effects. The particular brand of violence in Cooks may have been due to the effects of lead poisoning. Schoolteacher Carl Simmons, for example, was shot twice in the back as he entered the school. Joseph Eswell was shot and killed simply for suggesting that the lard another man was putting on his boots would not make them waterproof. It has even been suggested that the more outlandish "tales" in James McKenna's *Black Range Tales* were the result of McKenna being "leaded" in Cooks.

The silver panic of 1897 proved a temporary setback at the Cookes Peak mines, which by then had twelve producing mines shipping twenty tons of ore a day. Mine productivity gradually fell over the next twenty years as the supply of high-grade ore was being depleted. In 1953, the last year of mining at Cookes Peak, two tons of lead ore and nineteen ounces of silver were produced. The last resident left Cooks in 1959.

Today Hadley lies beyond a locked gate where a windmill works hard at filling a stock tank. A wooden shack, crushed nearly flat by its roof, seems to have fallen in one calamitous crash. A stone garage is losing its roof, while its wooden doors sway in the wind. Mine tailings nearby are a sulfurous shade of lime. The ruins of Cooks and Jose lie high on the mountain, but both are inaccessible and on private land.

Cookes Spring, however, makes up for the two "lost" towns. In 1889 the railroad covered the spring with a large stone building and piped water to its station at Florida. Today the low, circular spring house stands in a thicket of mesquite. The spring has been capped, but in the evening the air smells as musty as a cellar.

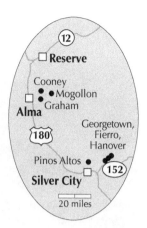

· 9 ·

The Mogollon:
Million-Dollar Mines

Pinos Altos · Hanover/Fierro · Georgetown ·
Graham · Cooney · Mogollon

Forty million years ago nature threw a tantrum in southwest New Mexico that sent volcanoes bursting through the overheated earth in a fury of fire, lava, and ash. For 15 million years these newborn mountains steamed and smoldered and blew again until they calmed and, under a covering of pine, finally settled down. Inside the mountains, though, lay the legacy of their frenzied past—turquoise, copper, gold, silver, iron, lead, manganese, molybdenum, selenium, and zinc.

The first to prospect the mountains were probably Mogollon Indians, who traded turquoise and copper nuggets to aboriginal customers as far away as Georgia. Spaniards picked up where the Indians left off and named the mountains Mogollon (Muggy-YOHN) after Juan Ignacio de Flores Mogollón. He was governor of New Mexico in the early 1700s and much interested in mining in the area.

In about 1801, José Manuel Carrasco began mining copper from a mountain noted for a monolith that resembled a kneeling nun. The landmark was called Santa Rita del Cobre—Santa Rita for the patron saint of stray flocks and *cobre* for "copper."

The Americans who arrived in the Mogollon in the nineteenth century searched the mountains for gold and silver. Once they made their strike, they set to making a business out of their good fortune. In a land as remote as the New Mexico Territory, that meant processing the ore on-site. To do this they used both ancient and, for the time, modern techniques.

From the Mexican miners, they adopted the *arrastra*. This ancient dragstone method of extraction used mule power to drag a 500-pound stone around the inside of a circular pit, in the process crushing the ore. The arrastra was simple and inexpensive and could be constructed on-site. But it was slow.

Threatening storm clouds hover over an elegant lineup of buildings—the south side of downtown Mogollon—that serve as a gateway to the vast and rugged Gila Wilderness Area.

From the California gold fields, they borrowed the stamp mill technique for crushing ore. The stamp was made up of five iron pestles, each weighing up to 350 pounds. They were attached to a steam-powered crankshaft that lifted and dropped the pestles to crush the ore. The stamp was expensive and had to be shipped from the East. But it could crush from one-and-a-half to three tons of rock in twenty-four hours.

However, for the mining towns of the Mogollon, their production days have long been over. Pinos Altos and Mogollon are two mining towns that once boomed heartily. The first lives quietly today as a mountain retreat, while the second is a place with a view. Graham is not a town at all but an outing, while Georgetown and Cooney are defined simply by their dead. Hanover and Fierro quit working not long ago by the looks of the rusted equipment by the road and the pulverized innards of a mountain piled high on the hillside.

Take NM 15 north from Silver City for 7 miles, then where the road divides keep left to Pinos Altos.

The Continental Divide zigzags through the heart of Pinos Altos, sending its creeks flowing either east or west according to their natures. The first two gold mines established here in 1860 were named the Atlantic and the Pacific for the destinations of their respective creeks.

Gold was first discovered in the area around 1837 by Mexican soldiers on the lookout for Indians. The troops were stationed at the Santa Rita outpost, where their duties included guarding the convict laborers at the copper mines. The first rush for gold began when three prospecting forty-niners stopped for supplies at the old Santa Rita fort, then headed on west.

Still a popular watering hole, The Buckhorn Saloon is well known for its charming 1865 atmosphere, good food, and weekend melodramas (complete with villains and popcorn to fling in their direction) performed in the attached Opera House.

Continuing on, they stopped at Bear Creek on May 18, 1860, where Henry Birch, leaning down to drink, found himself staring at *chispas*, small nuggets of gold in the creek bed. He scooped up a handful of nuggets, then all three men headed back to Santa Rita for mining supplies.

When they returned to what they would call Birchville, they were in the company of two brothers, Thomas and Virgil Mastin. Thomas Mastin established the Atlantic Mine there and set up the first arrastras for crushing ore. By the end of summer, they would be joined by 700 other men, all looking for gold.

The Mimbres Apaches, who occupied the pine mountains, saw the invasion of miners as a threat to their lands. Their chief, Mangas Coloradas, so named for his red shirt, was a tall, imposing leader already in his seventies when he joined with his son-in-law, Cochise, to drive out the miners. On the morning of September 22, 1861, their combined force of 400 warriors attacked the mining camp. The miners rallied under Thomas Mastin's command and battled the Apaches into the afternoon until the Indians retreated into the mountains. The fight left fifteen Apaches and three miners dead, including Thomas Mastin. The Apache chief had made his point.

Pinos Altos residents celebrate a turn-of-the-century summer with a "watermelon feed." Courtesy Silver City Museum, #3217.

The interior of "Mrs. Bell's parlor" in 1892 reflects the prosperity of Pinos Altos during that time. Nathaniel Bell's violin is shown propped on a chair. The parlor was on the Bell side of the Bell and Stephens family "duplex." Nathaniel Bell and Trolius Stephens were partners in the mining business. Courtesy Silver City Museum, #5853. Cecil Stephens Estate.

The next day, the miners began their exodus from Birchville, as well as from the camps at Santa Rita, San Jose, and Hanover. The Civil War was on, and many left to join either the Union or Confederate forces. The Mexican miners who stayed behind renamed the camp Pinos Altos for the "tall pines."

In January 1863, Mangas Coloradas, broken from his battle wounds, surrendered to Union soldiers at Pinos Altos. The troopers took him to an abandoned fort nearby and put him in jail. During the night, guards tortured him in his cell, prodding him with bayonets heated over a campfire. When the old chief flinched, the guards shot him for "attempting to escape." Cochise continued his raiding for another decade before his surrender in Arizona.

After the Civil War, miners returned to Pinos Altos in what one writer called a "second stampede." In July 1866 Virgil Mastin chartered the Pinos Altos Mining Company and erected the town's first stamp mill. The fifteen-stamp mill, weighing 700 pounds, was shipped from St. Louis by way of an ox-drawn wagon. In addition to the stamp mill, a sawmill and some seventy-five arrastras were in operation.

Pinos Altos was formally organized in 1868, complete with graded streets and four bridges across Bear Creek. The new town included some 700 residents, 120 houses, two stamp mills, two hotels, several stores, seven saloons, and a bathhouse. That year, Fort Bayard also was established ten miles away, ensuring the residents a measure of safety from Indian attack. Except for Virgil Mastin, who, that same year, was killed by Apaches outside of town.

Pinos Altos became the county seat for Grant County in 1869, but that designation proved to be short-lived. When an immense silver deposit was discovered at Bear Mountain, Silver City "sprang into existence as if by magic." The county seat was moved to this new boomtown in 1872.

Pinos Altos continued under a certain prosperity during the 1880s, with the Pacific Mine bringing in nearly $1 million during the decade. One booster observed that "throughout the town there is an air of thrift and prosperity." The town had a band, a baseball team, a Turkish bath, and a population of 1,000. Maple trees lined the streets (the pines having been sacrificed to the demands of the mines), and apple orchards flourished in backyard gardens. The number of saloons increased to fourteen, with "fancy ladies" coming from Silver City only on paydays. Chinese lived in the gulches around Pinos Altos, while Italian, Mexicans, and Cornishmen (miners from Cornwall, England) each claimed separate sections of town.

In 1887 George Hearst purchased most of the Pinos Altos Mining District. Hearst, a California mining tycoon and father of William Randolph Hearst, planned to build a narrow-gauge railroad linking the mines at Silver City, Pinos Altos, and Mogollon. Mrs. Hearst became involved in the effort to build a Methodist church in town, donating $500 to the cause. Phoebe Hearst insisted that the new church include a reading room, for which she agreed to pay the expenses. The Gold Avenue Methodist Church was dedicated on May 18, 1898.

The prosperity ebbed when the Hearst interests were sold in 1903. The railroad was dismantled before it was ever completed, and the church reading room closed. The sale effectively ended the productivity of the Pinos Altos gold mines, which during the era produced between $8 million and $10 million in gold.

Pinos Altos never became a ghost town and today still has a population of some 300. A log cabin built in 1866, which once served as a schoolhouse, now is the Pinos Altos Museum. It was built by a German miner who came to Pinos Altos in the 1860s. His great-great-grandson George Schaefer runs the museum, along with his mother, Frances Schaefer. The old Methodist church, now called the Hearst Church for its once-upon-a-time patron, houses the Grant County Art Guild. The courthouse is now a private residence, but the Buckhorn Saloon, built in 1865, is still in business. The neighboring Opera House as well as a scaled-down replica of the Santa Rita

The distinctive pitched roof of the Gold Avenue Methodist Church, now used as a community art gallery, pierces the deep blue mountain sky at Pinos Altos. Known as the Hearst Church for its benefactor, powerful California investor George Hearst, the 1880s structure is one of many remaining historic buildings in this old gold-mining town.

fort are of recent vintage. At the edge of town is the Church of the Holy Cross, built in 1888. Its cemetery contains the graves of Thomas and Virgil Mastin (misspelled as Marston on the tombstones).

The Pinos Altos Museum is open daily during summer and most weekends otherwise. (505) 388–1882

Hanover/ Fierro

Take NM 180 east from Silver City about 10 miles and turn north on NM 152. At the junction of NM 152 and NM 356 turn north and go 4 miles to Hanover. The Fierro Cemetery Road leads east across the railroad tracks at Fierro.

The making of Hanover and Fierro left behind props that even today could be used in a mining town movie. The story of the back-to-back towns begins with a prospector named Sofio Henkle, who came to the area from Hanover,

Miners stand on the tramway suspended above the road at the Empire Zinc Mine at Hanover in about 1925. The conveyor, which has since been removed, led the railroad tracks across the road. Courtesy Silver City Museum, #717.

Steep concrete steps lead to a false front, a roadside relic in Hanover, a town named for a location in Germany and famous for the striking miners and their wives who inspired *The Salt of the Earth.*

Germany, in 1841. When the Apaches drove him out two years later, all that remained was the name of his hometown. Fierro, Spanish for "iron," came by its name naturally.

Mining didn't begin in earnest until 1891, when iron and zinc were discovered at Hanover. That year rail lines reached Hanover Junction, six miles south of town. In 1899, William J. Palmer, a railroad builder and president of the Colorado Fuel and Iron Company, took the tracks to Hanover and on to Fierro. The mines shipped as many as ten carloads of ore a day to the company's steel mills in Pueblo, Colorado. During its lifetime, which ended with the Depression, Fierro mines alone produced 6 million tons of iron.

What iron had been to Fierro, zinc later would be to Hanover. During World War I the Empire Zinc Company established a mine and mill at Hanover. Throughout both world wars, the mine was a steady producer. It was the cold war, however, that would put Hanover in the spotlight—and in a movie—that to this day draws controversy.

On October 17, 1950, 140 miners went on strike against the Empire Zinc Company to end the "dual wage rates" in which Anglo miners were paid more than Hispanic miners for the same work. The miners also wanted an end to the policy of assigning the underground jobs only to Hispanic miners. Plus the miners complained that their company housing was inferior to that of the Anglo employees. The strikers were members of the International Union of Mine, Mill, and Smelter Workers, which championed racial equality but whose leadership also was suspected of being Communists.

What set the strike apart from other mine walkouts was the involvement of the miners' wives. Eight months into the strike, the Empire Zinc Company hired strikebreakers to replace the striking miners. To prevent confrontations between the strikebreakers and the picketing miners, a federal judge issued a restraining order prohibiting the men from picketing. The miners' wives then proposed to replace the men on the picket line, thus circumventing but not violating the judge's order. Soon the sheriff found himself faced with a "hoard of screaming, singing, chanting women and children." The sheriff jailed them all—sixty-two women and children, including a one-month-old baby. By evening the women were released and celebrating their newfound solidarity.

The women marched the picket line for seven months, often in the face of hostility. "Everybody had a gun, except us," one women recalled. "We had knitting needles. We had safety pins. We had straight pins. We had chile peppers. And we had rotten eggs."

The strike ended in January 1952, fifteen months after it began, with the miners winning a modest wage increase and life insurance and health benefits. They also got hot running water in their company houses.

Hillside homes of varying age lie in the shadow of mining activities at Fierro, which produced tons of the metal for which it was named—iron—until its demise during the Depression.

Salt of the Earth, the film based on the Empire Zinc strike, was released in 1954. Some scenes were filmed in Fierro (but not Hanover), and many of those who had a role in the strike played similar parts in the film. *Salt of the Earth* was written, directed, and produced by members of the Hollywood Ten, who had been blacklisted for refusing to testify before the House Un-American Activities Committee. The film, which was suppressed for decades, is now available on video.

And what of Hanover and Fierro? The railroad tracks still lead up Hanover Creek past the hulking remains of the Empire Zinc Mine. Along the way is the old grocery store, newly trimmed in green, the old train station, now the post office, and an old storefront shuttered in rusted tin. A small sign reading Historic Fierro announces its town limits. The road dead-ends near St. Anthony's Catholic Church, which according to the sign dates from 1860.

The Fierro Cemetery, which covers the steep hillside east of the canyon, is remarkable by mining town standards. It is large, well kept, and colorful. A Christ figure at the top of the cemetery towers over the graves at its feet, each grave decorated in bouquets of bright plastic. Many of the other graves are marked with tall, blue metal crosses.

Georgetown

Go east from Silver City on US 180 to the junction with NM 152. From this junction go 7 miles on NM 152 to the turnoff to Georgetown, which is directly across from the Kneeling Nun landmark and the Santa Rita open pit mine. Go north on the

The peaceful forested cemetery is all that marks the location of Georgetown. Once a bustling 1,200 residents strong, the town faded away due to a combination of deadly factors: a smallpox epidemic, a crash in silver prices, and the lack of a railroad spur to the mining community.

Mining in Georgetown was still a pick, hammer, and candle operation in 1900 (note candleholder on back wall). Courtesy Silver City Museum, #557. George Schaefer Collection.

> Old Georgetown Road (the dirt road is unmarked but runs
> alongside Santa Rita Park), passing a cemetery on the left
> (this is not the Georgetown Cemetery). At 1.1 miles, take the
> right fork. The Georgetown Cemetery is on the left 4 miles
> from the turnoff.

Georgetown once was the second-richest silver camp in New Mexico, but when Fayette Jones visited in 1903, he despaired at the sight of the dying town. Gone, he lamented, was the "throng of sturdy prospectors and miners" and the "incessant clattering" of the stamp mills. Long rows of empty buildings that "cast their ghostly shows by the lingering sun" filled him with "indescribable fear and horror." "Oh, what utter desolation!" he cried.

Jones was a little premature (and melodramatic) in reporting the demise of Georgetown, but not by much. That year, the railroad had laid tracks to Fierro but not on to Georgetown, three miles away but on the wrong side of the mountain. When that happened, the population dropped to 100. The population already had begun to dwindle when the mines and mills shut down, victims of the 1897 silver crisis.

But in 1888, Georgetown, a "nice, snug" town of 1,200 people, was at its peak. The town was laid out in a V shape. At its apex was a large spring that supplied the town its water. One arm of the V followed Willow Springs Canyon and was the residential side of town, where the churches, schools, and Georgetown's finer homes were built. From the spring, a second arm curved south, where the businesses—stores, saloons, the jail, and miners' shacks—found their places.

Silver was first discovered in the area in 1866, but the silver mines were not developed until 1872, when the Mimbres Mining and Reduction Company was founded by John Magruder and his brother George. The new town was named in honor of George, who was born in Georgetown, District of Columbia.

The mines at Georgetown yielded nearly pure silver, with the biggest deposits found close to the surface. Still, miners, mostly Cornishmen working by candlelight, cut some fifteen miles of tunnels into the mountains. The mines kept the two stamp mills on the Mimbres River operating at capacity twenty-four hours a day. In all, the mines at Georgetown produced $3.5 million in silver.

Graham

The Catwalk (Graham) is 5 miles from Glenwood on FSR 95. The road, marked Cat Walk, follows Whitewater Canyon.

Gold and silver were discovered in the mountains above Whitewater Canyon in 1889, leading to the development of several mines in its upper reaches. Although the waters of Whitewater Creek could be used to power a stamp mill, the canyon itself proved too narrow and too steep to accommodate a mill. John T. Graham solved the dilemma in 1893 by building a stamp mill at the mouth of the canyon, where the creek entered a wide, gentle valley. Graham, the town that grew up around the mill, at one time had about 200 people.

The location of the mill presented it own problem, however, because the creek's flow at the lower site was insufficient to power the mill's electric generator. The solution was to build a four-inch water pipe from the top of the canyon, where water was plentiful, to the mill three miles below. The pipeline, packed in sawdust and encased in wood to prevent it from freezing, ran along the canyon's north wall.

These men are trying to convince the wood-laden burro to cross Whitewater Creek. The sycamore trees along the creek were good sized even in 1911. Courtesy Silver City Museum, #717. Frank Skidmore Collection.

When a larger generator was installed at the mill in 1897, it required more water and thus a second water line. The new, eighteen-inch pipeline ran parallel to the smaller one. Iron bars anchored deep in the rock face held the timber supports for the water pipes. In places they were twenty feet above the canyon floor. Repairmen who walked the pipeline dubbed it the "catwalk."

While Graham's engineering was remarkable, his timing was not. The silver market crashed the same year he enlarged his mill. Graham was down to three families when the mine closed for good in 1913. In 1935 the Civilian Conservation Corp. built a wooden walkway they dubbed the "Catwalk" over the old pipeline route. The U.S. Forest Service replaced the wooden walkway with a metal one in the 1960s. These days it is the Catwalk that draws people to the rugged canyon.

I've hiked the Catwalk before, so today I'm taking a leisurely lunch before heading up the canyon. But the sun at my back and the creek's soothing lullaby have made me drowsy and a little lazy. Sycamore trees arching overhead rustle their big bear-paw leaves to catch my attention. The graceful giants

A worker stands on a pipeline under construction, probably in Whitewater Canyon. Courtesy Silver City Museum, #01613.

Clinging to the side of sheer canyon walls, the Catwalk of Whitewater Canyon in the Mogollon Mountains follows the twists and turns of this prized source of water that enabled the mill downstream at Graham to prosper.

remind me of a childhood Bible song about Zacchaeus, the "wee little man" who climbed a sycamore in order to see Jesus. Which then reminds of another tree story, the one played out in Whitewater Canyon in the winter of 1906.

It seems that a rancher known as Hannigan owed a cowboy named Bob Holliman $1,000 for ranch work. But when rancher Hannigan sold his spread without settling up with Holliman, the cowboy suspected the old man might skip town. Sure enough, the rancher was on the next midnight stage out of Mogollon. The cowboy jumped the stage when it reached Glenwood, took the rancher off at gunpoint, then sent the stage on its way. To hide Hannigan's tracks, the cowboy wrapped the old man's feet in gunnysacks and marched him up Little Whitewater Creek. There he chained the rancher to a big tree, leaving him with enough chain to reach the creek for water and a bag of hard sourdough biscuits to eat.

At daylight, the cowboy arrived at the Jones Brothers Store in Alma four miles away with a ransom note from Hannigan. The rancher instructed the Jones brothers to find the money to pay Holliman his $1,000, for which he promised to reimburse them. It took three days to scare up the cash. Once he had his money, the cowboy rode back to the creek, taking along an extra horse. He unchained his pitiful hostage from the ransom tree, then delivered him safely to Alma. The rancher, having learned his lesson, kept his promise to the Jones brothers. The law made a faint effort to apprehend Bob Holliman, who it was said already had left for California, riding the finest horse in the county.

In my daydreaming, I've nearly forgotten to look for the ruins of the old mill. I find them easily enough—three or four rocky foundations stacked one above the other on the hill north of the parking lot. Then I head for the Catwalk.

The Catwalk trail is 1 mile long. Parking $3. National Catwalk Recreation Area, (505) 539–2481.

Cooney

From Glenwood go north on US 180 toward Alma. At Alma, turn right on FSR 701, Mineral Creek Road. Take this dirt road 4.5 miles, taking the left fork at this point. Cooney's tomb is on the right less than half a mile from the fork and just past the cattle guard.

In 1870 Sergeant James C. Cooney arrived at Fort Bayard as part of a mapping expedition. The fort had been established to protect miners from the Indians, so Cooney certainly knew the mountains contained gold and silver. In 1875, while out mapping in the area, he found what he must have hoped for—silver and gold. He kept his discovery secret until his enlistment was up the next year, then established his claim, the Silver Bar, along what would come to be called Mineral Creek.

From the beginning, the Cooney Mining District was beset by Indians. On April 28, 1880, Victorio and his Apaches attacked Cooney's camp, killing four miners and burning the cabins. The remaining miners retreated to Alma. There they joined several settlers holed up at John Roberts's place, a log cabin fortified inside the Alma stockade. Apaches circled the fortress for a day and night, shooting only the one poor soul who peeked out the cabin door. At daybreak the Indians left. James Cooney and William Chick then decided to ride back to Cooney to check on the mines and to look for survivors. They were ambushed and killed just outside the mining camp, and both were buried there by the road.

After Cooney's death, his brother Michael Cooney took over the mine.

Entombed in an enormous boulder, the final resting place of James Cooney, who was attacked and killed by Apache warriors in 1880, marks the general location of the flood-ravaged town that bore his name.

Later Michael created a shrine for his fallen brother near where James had been killed. Michael blasted a hole in a rough boulder, interred his brother inside the rock tomb, then sealed it with ore from the Silver Bar Mine.

By 1889, some 600 people lived at Cooney's camp, which included three stamp mills, a school, a church, and two hotels. The store at Cooney sold everything from groceries, to made-to-order men's suits, to coffin handles. In September 1911, a flood swept through Cooney, destroying most of its buildings, including the mine plant and mill. In 1914, Michael Cooney, then in his seventies, froze to death while looking for a lost mine in Sycamore Canyon. He is buried in Socorro.

Today only Cooney's tomb survives, its entrance sealed in stones streaked with turquoise and iron. It sits close to the road, with brush and oak trees at its back. Behind the tomb, three graves rest in a tiny plot edged in lichen-covered stones. Another grave lies inside an iron fence but is missing its tombstone. Some say it is William Chick's.

An office assistant at his typewriter outside a mine office in Cooney in about 1912. Courtesy Silver City Museum, #05134.

Mogollon

From Glenwood drive north on US 180 for 4 miles, then take NM 174 east for 9.2 miles to Mogollon. The road is one lane the last 5 miles, so honk at hairpin curves. To reach the Mogollon Cemetery, turn left at the wooden church on the hill at the east end of town. The road quickly makes a hard left going past the fire station, then heads up a steep, rocky hill. The 1-mile climb (which requires a high-clearance vehicle) ends at a T. The gated entrance to the Little Fanny Mine is to the left, but a sign warns against even walking this route. The road to the right leads to the cemetery.

It takes two to go to Mogollon, one to drive and one to take in the scenery. Since I am the lucky passenger, today I get to be the tourist.

The road to Mogollon climbs out of the narrow river valley and onto Whitewater Mesa, a perfectly flat shelf covered in amber grass. Its open edge provides an unbroken view of the far mountains, dappled in the shadow of clouds on the move. The panorama is left behind as the road scrambles on up the mountain. A high tight curve brings into view the next scenic spot—the Little Fanny Mine, its chalky tailings spilling down the hillside. Then suddenly the road takes a dive, doubles back on itself, then dives again, rounds a corner, and ends up on Main Street, Mogollon.

Now imagine making the trip, a climb of 2,000 feet in seven miles, with a team of eighteen horses pulling a freight wagon filled with tons of mining equipment. The ride was worth the effort because the mines at Mogollon were worth millions. Eventually the Mogollon Mining District would produce $15 million in minerals—gold, silver, and copper.

Mogollon dates from 1889, when an old prospector named John Eberle struck it rich with the Last Chance Mine at Silver Creek. His cabin at the foot of Silver Creek Canyon became the first building in what would become Mogollon. His strike came just as the mines at Cooney, three miles across the mountain, began to give out. Within weeks miners were deserting Cooney for Mogollon.

Although Silver Creek Canyon was a poor location for a town, its residents seemed not to mind. Mogollon was wedged at the base of a deep, narrow canyon and shared a good part of its main street with the creek coursing down its middle. Wooden buildings crowded along both sides of the creek. The buildings on the north bank of the creek came with their own footbridges.

By 1892, Mogollon had a post office, a school, and a jail. Harry Hermann, who owned the lumber mill, donated the wood for a proper jail. Before that, troublemakers were simply tied to a tree. When the town celebrated the jail's completion, Hermann got so drunk he was arrested for disturbing the peace and thrown into his own jail.

In 1894, Mogollon suffered the first in a lifelong cycle of fire and flood. After the first fire destroyed most of its wooden buildings, the town rebuilt with adobe and stone. Most of those buildings were spared in the later fires. Melting snow and spring rains swept down the mountain in five successive floods. In the flood of 1914, a downpour saturated the tailings dump at the Little Fanny Mine and sent the slurry sliding down the mountain in a swath half a mile wide. The slurry took out the timbers of the Maude S. Mine, burying its sleeping watchman in its wake. As if flood and fire weren't plague enough, the flu epidemic of 1918 killed fifty-two of Mogollon's residents.

Regardless of disaster, the mines at Mogollon kept on producing. The era of its greatest prosperity began with the development of the Little Fanny Mine in 1909. By 1913, some 2,000 people lived in the remote canyon along Silver Creek. That year alone gold and silver production from mines such as the Little Fanny, Champion, McKinley, Pacific, and Deadwood reached $1.5 million. Mogollon had a theater, an icehouse, and a bakery, plus a school with 300 students, a Catholic and a Presbyterian church, and a hospital with

Wooden footbridges still provide access across Silver Creek to the south-facing buildings on Mogollon's main street, including the renovated J. P. Holland General Store establishment, which provides bed-and-breakfast lodging today.

three physicians. But it also had plenty of saloons, two red-light districts, and more than its measure of violence for a twentieth-century town.

Although Mogollon was a late bloomer by mining town standards, it still practiced the vices common to the mining towns of the late 1800s. Robbers held up the stage to Silver City in 1910, killing the driver and stealing the bullion on board. Two Mexican bandits stole $14,000 from the payroll office in 1912 and killed a clerk and his assistant. Drunks were still shooting up the bars in 1917, and Prohibition was routinely ignored in Mogollon's saloons during the 1920s.

By World War I, Mogollon's wild days were over. Demand for gold and silver was down, production costs were up, and the mines were nearly played out. By 1930, Mogollon's population dipped to 300. Then in 1934, when the price of gold went from $20 to $35 an ounce, Mogollon temporarily revived and its population jumped to 1,000. But by World War II, demand dropped again and a devastating fire in 1942 ended Mogollon's mining town life for good.

Today about fifteen people live in Mogollon year-round. Summers bring a steady stream of tourists who take the wild ride up the mountain to see what's left of Mogollon. Most of Main Street's stone buildings have survived. Footbridges still cross the creek to buildings on its north bank. The town has two museums and a couple of fake movie set buildings. But an old log cabin with a fairly new tin roof looks authentic, as do many small wood cabins weathered a tobacco brown. Two 1920s-era automobiles, both missing their engines, sit rusting next to a vintage gas pump.

Mogollon still must have a certain unwanted element (tourists?) since the place is plastered with No Trespassing, Private Property, and Do Not Touch signs. One property is laced in concertina wire.

At the top of the hill where the road splits one way to the Little Fanny, a sign warns sternly against any thoughts of trespassing. We take the other road to the cemetery and are justly rewarded. Dozens of iron fences mark family plots, while other graves bear an array of iron crosses and decorative tombstones. A large Celtic cross stands at the head of a family plot that is undergoing renovation. Spanish dagger, alligator juniper, and knee-high weeds govern the cemetery without the aid of a sign.

Indian Artifact Museum and Mogollon Museum.

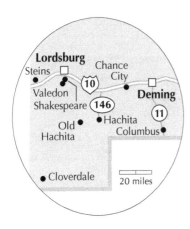

· 10 ·

The Bootheel:
Hard Country

Chance City · Shakespeare · Valedon·Steins ·
Cloverdale · Old Hachita · Hachita · Columbus

I live on an acre of Chihuahuan Desert, so I know that green comes in shades of olive and brown, that wind can drive you mad, and that heat can give you headaches. I know to watch for rattlesnakes in September and scorpions all summer long. But out here I can also see a million stars at night and the full sweep of sunset in winter. From my back porch I can watch a dozen quail on parade and a skinny lizard taking lunch. Once in a while a fox will visit, sniffing around, taking his time.

But even by my own reckoning, the desert I share with New Mexico's Bootheel is mighty hard country. No part of the state is as hot or seems as windy as this borderland corner. It gets less than a dozen inches of rain a year and evaporates it all back and then some. Its creeks tend to seep underground, and its one river never connects with another. Its lakes are crusty playas—salty mudflats that fill only when it rains. By New Mexico standards, its four mountain ranges are neither high nor remarkable. Even the Apaches were tougher here, the last battlegrounds of Geronimo, Cochise, and Victorio.

What, then, draws people to "the loneliest land that ever came out of God's hands"? Mary Austin, writing in 1903, posed the question and the answer. "There is promise there of great wealth in ores and earths. . . . Men are bewitched by it and tempted to try the impossible."

Trailblazers were the first to recognize the value of the basin-and-range landscape for its warm winter passage. Colonel Philip St. George Cooke routed his wagon road through here on his way to California in 1846. Although the area was Mexican territory, the United States all along had coveted it for a railroad route to the Pacific. Then in 1853, a railroad executive named James Gadsden was appointed as minister to Mexico. Gadsden arrived to find Santa Ana's government on the verge of bank-

Maybe a survivor of the Steins Peak Butterfield Stage stop, this stagecoach is right at home at the privately owned Steins Railroad Ghost Town, where adobe and wood buildings are furnished with artifacts from the 1880s community.

ruptcy, so he offered Santa Ana a solution to his financial woes—sell part of Mexico's northern territories to the United States. Under terms of the 1854 Gadsden Treaty the United States paid Mexico $10 million for a 30,000-square-mile strip of land from south of the Gila River to the present Mexican border and all the way to California. The treaty secured much more than a railroad route, for within the Gadsden Purchase lay copper, silver, and gold.

Today the Bootheel mines have given out, the railroad has pulled up its tracks, and most of the towns have been abandoned. Some survive as living history museums, while others have fallen to their rocky knees. A store is all that's left of a ranch community, and an old hotel bears the scars of a wartime raid. Mary Austin's benediction of a century ago still holds for this hard country. "For all the toll the desert takes of a man it gives compensations, deep breaths, deep sleep, and the communion of the stars."

Chance City

Chance City is not on any map, but it is easy to find. Take exit 62 on I-10, 20 miles west of Deming. Turn south under the interstate and travel 2.2 miles on the paved road that passes alongside the Bowlin Travel Center. Then take the dirt road for 1.5 miles to the ruins. Watch for cattle on the road.

The monsoon season has come and gone, leaving behind buttery flowers spilling onto the dirt road. From their summer soaking, the low hills of the Victorio Mountains have grown a down of green. In darker shades, the hillside is dotted with slender yucca, chunky juniper, and creosote bushes showing tiny yellow blooms. It is a perfect day in Chance City.

It is surprising to see so much left of Chance City since the map shows only mining symbols in place of a town. True, it was no Pinos Altos, but it was one of George Hearst's mining ventures.

The rock-and-adobe skeletal remains of Chance City blend with the rough landscape from which they were created on a sunny hillside of the Victorio Mountains.

Three prospectors found silver in the Victorio Mountains in about 1880 but soon sold their claims to the partnership of George Hearst, Lloyd Tevis, and James Ben Ali Haggin. Hearst was a miner and geologist from California who it was said could "smell gold or silver." His partners—and backers—were former lawyers from San Francisco who saw more opportunity as land speculators and mining promoters.

The Chance Mine, whose shaft ran 200 feet inside the mountain, produced lead, silver, and some gold. The mining camp that grew up at the mine was at first called Victorio but later became Chance City. By 1883 some 130 people, miners and their families, lived at Chance City. But in 1886, when the price of lead dropped, the mines closed. Although the mines at Chance City were short-lived, they produced $1.5 million in ore and spurred the partners toward other ventures, such as the Homestake Mine in South Dakota and the mines at Pinos Altos. Hearst also used his fortune to buy the *San Francisco Examiner*, which he later turned over to his son William Randolph Hearst, and to buy the Diamond A Ranch, today's Gray Ranch, in New Mexico's Bootheel.

Chance City today shows its roots as a simple mining town. There is no saloon, no jail, no church, no school, no old-timer to tell the tale. Instead, there are seven structures of adobe and stone, all without roofs and most lacking four walls. Near the road a skeletal head frame stands over a shaft sealed for safety. On the hill above, a wooden chute's timbers mark a dark, open mine shaft.

Chance City is also good reason never to go to a ghost town alone. While most of the mine shafts are covered in grates, others high on the hill may not be. At least two tunnels show signs of cave-in. One gaping hole exposes the timbers below and could be a rattlesnake hideout. A fall into any one of these could ruin an otherwise perfect day in Chance City.

Shakespeare

At Lordsburg, take exit 22 on I-10. Go south on the paved road for 1.2 miles, then just before the cemetery turn west onto a dirt road and go 1 mile to Shakespeare. Stop by the cemetery on the way back out.

Shakespeare is on fire. Roaring, wind-whipped flames use their mad energy in trying to destroy the town. The fire has not yet finished with the blacksmith shop before heading to the store next door, its flames carried on the cruel wind. A man and woman fight against the fire. The store is their home, the town their own. His face and hands are burned. She is uncommonly beautiful. It is April 10, 1997.

❧

Shakespeare began as a watering hole at the base of the Pyramid Mountains and was frequented by Apaches and Mexican herders. By the time Cooke's Mormon Battalion took their wagon road through here in 1846, it was known as Mexican Springs. Mexican Springs was first settled in about 1856 and was as an alternate stop on the Butterfield Stage route until the Civil War put an end to the line.

The new company that took over the Butterfield route after the war refurbished the former stage stop and renamed it Pyramid after the mountains. But its stationmaster, John Evanson, thought it more fitting to name the stage stop in honor of General Ulysses S. Grant, the popular hero of the Civil War. So Grant it was, population, two.

This name might have stuck if it weren't for a surveyor working on the U.S.-Mexico boundary line who also spent time poking around the Pyramid Mountains. W.D. Brown found silver so pure that he quit his job and took his ore sample all the way to California to be assayed. When it assayed at 12,000 ounces of silver to the ton, Brown went in search of a backer. He found it in William Chapman Ralston.

Ralston was the founder of the Bank of California. He entertained lavishly at his 100-room mansion in San Francisco and invested heavily in everything from real estate, to horses, to mining. By March 1870, Ralston's New Mexico Mining Company was staking claims in Grant. The company laid out a town with wide parallel streets, filled it with tents and a few buildings, then renamed it Ralston. Within a year, the town had 174 residents. Meanwhile, Ralston was selling stock in the company all over the United States but mainly in Europe.

Other miners hurried to stake claims in the new mining district but arrived to find that Ralston's company already owned the best claims. The prospectors also found these claims under the guard of the Company Boys, tough gunmen from Texas who had hired on with Ralston. When the company realized that the mountains held just a few pockets of silver, it quietly shut down its operation, leaving the Company Boys on guard.

Coincidently, two prospectors showed up at the Bank of California with diamonds they claimed they found in the Pyramid Mountains. Ralston sent a few of the diamonds to Tiffany's, where they appraised at $150,000. When his mining expert confirmed the diamond field, Ralston bought out the two prospectors. Then he formed a new outfit—the New York Mining and Commercial Company—and once more took to selling stock. Back at camp, the Company Boys were showing around a cigar box full of diamonds they

The Stratford Hotel, where a young Billy the Kid is reported to have washed dishes, is the background for members of the Paso del Norte Pistoleros during a reenactment. The group, along with the Friends of Fort Selden, provide living history demonstrations to visitors four times a year and also help maintain and restore Shakespeare's old buildings.

said they found in the mountains. Prospective stockholders even found a few diamonds sparkling from an anthill there. The *San Francisco Chronicle* reported on August 1, 1872, that every share of Ralston's first stock offering was snapped up in a day.

By the end of that summer, 3,000 people had flocked to Ralston, all hoping to find silver *and* diamonds. The true moneymakers, though, were the businesses that popped up to serve the hopefuls. Ralston had a barbershop, a hotel, boardinghouses, restaurants, seven saloons, a Chinese laundry, an assay office, and a red-light district. And it had the Company Boys to enforce the law. What it didn't have was a school, or a church, or a bank—or any diamonds.

The diamond frenzy attracted the attention of a government geologist named Clarence King, who decided to investigate the strike. King's investigation showed that the diamond field had been "salted" with Brazilian and African diamonds. Ralston and the company claimed to be victims of the hoax. While some believed that Ralston was innocent, others in the company made off with a fortune, including the diamond "prospectors." On August 27, 1875, a day after his bank failed, Ralston took a dip in San Francisco Bay and drowned.

By then only a few souls remained in the town of Ralston, including John Evanson, the old stationmaster, and a few out-of-work Company Boys, who hung out there. Some of these Texans took up ranching, using cattle rustled from Mexico to stock their spreads. All in all, Ralston had earned its bad name.

In 1879 John Boyle, a St. Louis investor and Shakespearean scholar, and his partner, William Boyle, an Irish-born mining engineer, filed on old claims in the Pyramid Mountains. They gave the place the literary name of

Janaloo Hill, who inherited the primitive cluster of adobe buildings in southwestern New Mexico known today as Shakespeare, is pictured in period dress in front of the 1870s Assay Office. The ghost town is open for tours several times a year, which are led by Hill, her husband, Manny Hough, and volunteers.

Shakespeare and started over. Not to pass up a good thing, John named Shakespeare's hotel the Stratford and its thoroughfare Avon Avenue. The town still had its rough characters, its gunfights, and a hanging or two, but its name remained untarnished.

When the railroad established the new town of Lordsburg three miles away, it eclipsed Shakespeare. The silver crisis of 1897 sent the town into decline. As the residents moved away, they dismantled their houses down to the very timbers, taking along what they could use. The town had a brief reprieve in 1907, when some of the old claims were reopened west of Shakespeare at Valedon, but by 1932 the Depression had closed all the mines and Shakespeare was not much more than an old stage stop.

In 1935 a lanky cowboy named Frank Hill and his pretty wife, Rita, bought Shakespeare. Frank had come to New Mexico from Texas in 1913 because, he said, "Texas got too tame." Rita had been a dancer and an extra in silent films and a schoolteacher. They had already lost one ranch to the Depression, but they were game for a second try. The previous owner had thought Shakespeare would be a good tourist attraction, but he never saw the idea through.

Rita and Frank had a ranch to run—horses and cattle on 11,000 acres—and a daughter to raise. Janaloo Hill, as her mother said, turned out to be "photogenic" as well as gifted with her mother's dramatic flair. She was raised in Shakespeare in a house that had once been the town's mercantile. She left for a time, off to college, then to New York, Los Angeles, and Denver, where she worked as a model and an actress. Janaloo came home in the mid-1960s. "It just seemed like I was needed here, so I came back and stayed," she said. She helped with the ranch, and for thirty years she and her mother taught dance, first in Lordsburg, then at their studio in Shakespeare.

The two actresses, mother and daughter, wrote a one-woman play depicting the women who lived at Shakespeare during its long history. Janaloo performed the skits for visitors to the old ghost town. Frank Hill died in 1970 and Rita Hill in 1985. Janaloo and her husband, Manny Hough, continued to run the ranch and the ghost town. They had remodeled their mercantile-home just before the 1997 fire. Gone in that fire were three buildings, including their home, all their personal belongings, plus Janaloo's library of rare books and costumes.

❧

It is August 25, 2001. Janaloo Hill is in costume, dressed in a long, pale blue dress trimmed in lace, a cameo at her neck. Against the sun she wears a matching bonnet—and sunglasses. Her guests, fourteen tourists and an unruly dog, follow her from building to building while she tells the story of

Shakespeare. She looks fragile and a little wilted in the 100-degree heat. But she does not waver.

Shakespeare is on the National Register of Historic Places. The ghost town is open for tours some weekends, with living history performances four times a year. Fee. (505) 542-9034; www.shakespeareghostown.com

Valedon

Where the road forks at the entrance to the Shakespeare RV parking lot, take the left fork for half a mile up a hill on a crumbling paved road (washed out in places). The road ends at a gate to a private gravel operation. Use binoculars to view Valedon from here.

Valedon (locals pronounce it VALE-don) got its start when Sam Ransom, a blacksmith from Shakespeare, and two partners filed claims in the Pyramid Mountains. The year was 1885. The spot where they found silver became known as '85 Hill and their claim, the '85 Mine. The '85 Mine languished under several owners until about 1913, when the Eighty-Five Mining Company took over production.

At first the workers lived in Lordsburg and walked the five miles to Valedon, cutting a path through Shakespeare. Ore wagons coming from the mine followed the same route back to the Southern Pacific Railroad station at Lordsburg. When the railroad built a spur line to Valedon, it laid tracks straight through Shakespeare's main street, leading the residents there to complain about trains "chugging through at any and all hours." The pedestrian miners walked the tracks to Valedon, stopping off at the saloons in Shakespeare on the way home.

As production stepped up at the '85, Henry Clay, and Atwood mines, the company built a mill to process the gold, silver, and copper ores. Workers began building houses at Valedon proper on land leased from the mining company. They used water flowing from the '85 Mine to irrigate their lawns, flower gardens, and orchards. By 1926, some 2,000 people lived in Valedon, now a company town that included the '85 Store, a meat market, a theater, and a blacksmith shop. Shakespeare's saloons and hotels apparently proved sufficient as Valedon built none of its own. It did have a large two-room school, which also served students from Lordsburg.

For a time Valedon prospered under company ownership. But in 1931 the Phelps Dodge Company bought the property and, a year later, with little warning, shut down the mine and ordered the residents to leave. The houses

Tucked into the side of a pock-marked mountain, the mining town of Valedon is off-limits to visitors but can be viewed from the top of a neighboring hill. The community, about three miles south of Lordsburg, thrived for several decades after the mines around neighboring Shakespeare played out.

were torn down, and many of the company buildings were moved to other locations. Almost overnight Valedon became a "place of ruined walls and hopes," Rita Hill wrote in her history of Shakespeare.

It's true. All that is left of Valedon today are the walls of the company store and the school.

Steins

Steins is 20 miles west of Lordsburg at exit 3 on I-10 and 4 miles east of the Arizona state line.

Any visit to this easygoing ghost town has to begin with a lesson on how Steins got its name. Let's make it simple.

Let's agree that Steins (pronounced locally as STEENS) was named for Major Enoch Steen of the U.S. Army, whose troops camped in the area in 1856. Some say the major died at the hands of Apaches in Doubtful Canyon, a deadly pass through the Peloncillo Mountains. In truth, Major Steen died of natural causes a quarter century later. Let's blame the Butterfield Stage for changing the spelling to Steins, for that is how it showed up in 1858, when the company named its Doubtful Canyon stage stop Steins Peak Station. Then let's forget about Steins, the stage stop in the canyon, and instead visit Steins, the railroad town on the highway.

Steins was founded in 1880 as a work station for the Southern Pacific Railroad, which in the space of a year laid tracks from California east to the Gulf of Mexico. Chinese laborers came through first, putting down gravel beds in preparation for the track layers who followed. By October, the train was serving the new town of Lordsburg, twenty miles east of Steins.

Boards sag under the weight of an old bottle collection at Steins—a historic location one recent visitor declared "spooky" because, she said, "it looks like all the residents just left their belongings one day and never came back."

Railroad workers at Steins lived in houses made of rough-cut lumber, adobe, and salvaged railroad ties. Since there was no water supply, they collected rainwater in barrels or bought water hauled from Doubtful Canyon at $1 a barrel.

The town boomed in 1905 when the railroad built a rock-crushing plant in the Peloncillo Mountains and a depot at Steins. This quarry provided crushed rock for 300 miles of railroad bed, nearly a third of the Southern Pacific's 1,000-mile route. The Chinese who worked at the quarry were not allowed to live in Steins and so were housed at the site. About 100 people lived in Steins, which by then had a post office, a store, a two-story hotel, and a saloon. Its population peaked at 200 just before the quarry shut down in the 1920s. The railroad closed its station at Steins in the 1950s, and its depot was moved to Cotton City, several miles south in the Animas Valley. Many of the buildings burned in a 1962 fire.

When Larry and Linda Link bought Steins in 1988, it was a "ten-acre junkyard," Linda says. Fortunately, many of the buildings were intact, and the junkyard yielded a treasure of railroad-era relics. Locals also donated many items original to Steins. From this conglomeration, the Links have created a homey, compact ghost town chock-full of history.

The town consists of ten wood and adobe buildings, all furnished according to their purposes and all wearing an authentically thin layer of dust. A bathhouse, for example, comes complete with claw foot tub, basin, and toilet. "Guard roosters" penned near the seamstress cabin announce the presence of wanted and unwanted visitors alike. One room of a two-crib bordello is furnished with a bed, a dresser, and a can of "Knock 'Em Dead Great Bed Bug Killer."

Linda Link, who runs the small store, complete with potbellied stove and soda machine, is the town's congenial historian. In a corral outside, two tiny pygmy goats are play-butting each other, under the bored gaze of a donkey named Bob. The goats, the donkeys, and the busybody chickens, Linda says, are historically accurate of early day Steins.

Steins Railroad Ghost Town. Fee. (505) 542–9791

Cloverdale

The route to Cloverdale begins 11 miles west of Lordsburg on I-10. Take exit 11 and go south for 25 miles on NM 338, a paved road. It becomes C1, a well-maintained dirt road, washboard in places. Keep going south on this road for 22 miles (do not take any forks), where it ends at Cloverdale.

Know this. When you reach Cloverdale, you will see only an adobe store stuffed with hay and under the patrol of a squadron of yellow jackets. But also know that the road to Cloverdale travels through a valley that in these parts passes for Eden.

The Animas Valley lies between two mountain ranges in a shallow plain once filled by an ancient lake. The playas at the north end of the valley are the dying remnants of this ice age lake, which a million years ago measured fifty feet deep but today measures only inches.

Leaving the dead seas behind, the road heads south into a greener landscape. Near a place called Cotton City, chile pickers work rows of green chiles. Farther on, acres of corn and sorghum look nearly ready for harvest. These fields are irrigated from groundwater pumped from below the surface—the legacy of the ancient lake.

Credit for the greening of this valley also goes to a phenomena known as a geothermal "hot spot." Ranchers had long noticed that after a snow, the accumulation on a quarter-acre patch of land near Cotton City melted immediately. From the air pilots also noticed that the patch was the first to green up in spring. The mystery was solved in 1948 when a well drilled at the spot produced *steam.* The water registered 240 degrees, making it the hottest well in New Mexico. The unique "hot spot" led to the discovery of a geothermal field underlying nearly a third of the county.

The landscape changes again as the route parallels Animas Creek, the Bootheel's part-time stream. Lofty cottonwoods are introduction to the rolling grasslands that soon follow. The grass is at first a thin cover for the rocky soil, then farther south grows taller and thicker, a savannah easily mistaken for Africa. When the road leaves the water route, it crosses a high meadow where monarch butterflies heading for Mexico pick and choose among wildflowers and pale grasses. A wooden sign on the road announces Cloverdale, fifteen feet away.

In 1880, when Michael Gray and his two sons established a ranch here, his son John Gray described it as "a big green meadow of about a thousand acres which was at the time covered with red top clover and watered by numerous springs." Gray had paid Curly Bill Graham, a gun-toting cattle rustler, $300 for his squatter's claim to the ranch. The next year, when Gray's younger son was killed in the Guadalupe Canyon massacre, Gray moved his family to Arizona. Gray, however, continued to "occupy" the ranch in order to prove up his claim. On November 20, 1883, a month after he received legal deed to the ranch at Cloverdale, he sold it to George Hearst and his partners for $12,000. Hearst, who had interests in land and mining development as well as publishing, was the father of William Randolph Hearst.

With the purchase, Hearst, who it was said "saw opportunity in all that free grass," established the Victorio Land and Cattle Company. The ranch

A one-building ghost town today, Cloverdale was established as a ranching community in New Mexico's lonely Bootheel country. It is surrounded by the lush grasslands of the Gray Ranch, purchased by the Nature Conservancy and now privately owned by a family dedicated to preserving its natural beauty and resources.

itself came to be known by its cattle brand, the Diamond A. The Diamond A Ranch would remain under company ownership for the next eighty years and eventually would include 510 square miles of land, about half the size of Rhode Island.

Cloverdale dates to about 1895, when a small store was established here some ten miles south of the Gray Ranch headquarters. The store sold goods to homesteaders and Diamond A cowboys alike. By 1913 Cloverdale had its own post office and a school through eighth grade. The school served students from Animas Valley ranches as well as one boy who rode his horse up from Mexico. The school burned in 1926 and was never rebuilt. The post office closed in 1943.

Cloverdale perhaps is best known for its Cowboy Picnic. The picnic was first held in 1919 to honor soldiers returning from World War I. As many as 150 people attended the annual event. Every July, cowboys and ranch families gathered at Cloverdale for a barbeque, horse racing, and a Saturday night dance. The Cloverdale Picnic was discontinued sometime after World War II, partly because it attracted too many outsiders.

In 1990 the Nature Conservancy bought the Gray Ranch for a reported $18 million as part of its "Last Great Places" campaign. The conservancy in turn sold the ranch to the Animas Foundation, a nonprofit group that manages the ranch under the philosophy that wildlife is part of the ranch's landscape. As such, the ranch is home not only to cattle, but also to seventy-five species of mammals, 247 species of resident and migrating birds, and 120 kinds of butterflies and moths.

The Cloverdale store, however, is home only to yellow jackets.

Old Hachita

The turnoff to Old Hachita is 4.9 miles west of Hachita on NM 9. The turnoff is unmarked and gated; however, the gate is not locked. Follow this dirt road, ignoring all the forks along the way, for 1.6 miles. At this point a rougher road branches off to the right, while the main road continues south. Take the right branch, which immediately forms a Y. One leg of the Y heads directly west for half a mile to Old Hachita. The other leg of the Y veers southwest to the American Mine site about a mile away. The rougher roads require a high-clearance vehicle.

In ancient times the Indians who mined turquoise in this small mountain range left behind tools, including stone pickaxes that hinted at the mountain's treasures. Spaniards must have discovered these mining tools—but not the treasures—for a 1762 Spanish map records the range as Sierra de la Hacha, "mountains of the ax."

In 1877 A.H. Butterfield found copper and silver in these mountains, and soon other miners were staking claims in the Eureka Mining District. The district's mining camp, also called Eureka, was soon a town with a general store, a couple of saloons, a boardinghouse, an assay office, and a blacksmith shop. A few of Eureka's residents built sturdy stone houses, while others made do with tents and shanties.

In 1882, Eureka had a population of 300 and its own post office. Along with the post office came the requirement for a new name (Eureka lacking originality). The town took the name Hachita, "little hatchet," for the mountains at its back. John Weems, who owned a store in Separ twenty miles to the north,

The shell of the stone blacksmith shop in Old Hachita is bordered by a "road" that leads to the adobe-and-rock ruins of this rough mining town, first founded as Eureka in an area where American Indians mined turquoise.

operated a stage line between Hachita and Separ. The stage brought mail and passengers three times a week, the mail for free, passengers for $3 a trip.

Hachita was vulnerable to raiding Apaches and every sort of outlaw chasing along the border. Three men who rode with Black Jack Ketchum's gang killed a U.S. Customs man not far from Hachita. At Separ two gunmen robbed the Weems store. Hachita, back when it was Eureka, was itself said to have been the center of a counterfeiting operation, with swindlers using the phony money to buy cattle in Mexico.

The mines were exhausted by the mid-1890s and the town's population dwindled to twenty-five. The railroad dealt Hachita a final blow in 1899 when it bypassed the town in favor of a route through the Hachita Valley. The new railroad town to the east took Hachita's name and its post office as well. Although some of the mines were worked into the 1940s, Old Hachita was never again a true town.

Unlike many abandoned mining towns, Old Hachita has not been stripped of its identity. Instead, its buildings have been left to fall apart of their own accord. One large structure, possibly a mine office, is shorn of all but one of its pink-and-green-striped metal awnings. The other awnings, fallen heavy to the ground, have taken their window frames with them. A large stone building under a threadbare roof might have been the blacksmith shop.

There is no doubt about the purpose of the buildings at the American Mine site. A head frame sits on a hill, its heavy timbers fallen at all angles. One large building is missing its roof and most of its walls, providing an open view of the ore-processing equipment rusting on its floor. Unlike Old Hachita, though, this site is fraught with hazards. Heavy timbers look ready to spill down the hillside, while a gaping hole near the head frame could mean disaster. Then there is the suspicious character staked out on the hill, his bright yellow truck a home office for both him and a couple of wary-looking dogs.

An extensive collection of rusting machinery remains in an ore-processing building at the American Mine site, which rests over the hill and south of Old Hachita.

Hachita is 45 miles west of Columbus on NM 9.

By the time Hachita was granted a post office in 1902, the town was already well established at the junction of two copper mine railroads. Here the Arizona and New Mexico Railroad, hauling copper ore from Morenci, Arizona, joined the El Paso and Southwestern Railroad, a border-hugging line going from the mines at Douglas, Arizona, to the refineries in El Paso, Texas.

Hachita at first was intended only as a water stop, but by the time the railroads built a depot, a freight warehouse, houses for the railroad officials, and a bunkhouse and restaurant for layover crews, they nearly had a town anyway. Soon miners in the Hachita Mountains were bringing wagonloads of ore for shipping. Cattle ranchers along both sides of the U.S.-Mexico border drove their cattle to the stockyards at Hachita. During fall roundup, tens of thousands of cattle were shipped out by rail, making Hachita one of the largest cattle-shipping points in the territory.

By 1912, Hachita had a population of about 700 and all the elements of a proper town, including a school and two churches. The Hachita Mercantile carried everything from food and clothing to guns and windmills. Each day the railroad brought the mail and daily newspapers from El Paso and Douglas.

In August of that year, Hachita's population doubled when a caravan of 800 Mormons arrived in town. The refugees had fled Colonia Diaz, their Mormon community in Mexico eighty miles south of Hachita, after Mexican revolutionaries murdered three of their members. When Mexican land reformers began seizing their livestock and property, the Mormons abandoned their colony and headed for the United States.

Hachita's residents lined the streets, watching as a U.S. Customs rider led the wagons through town to a treeless plain east of Hachita. There the U.S. Army had set up a refugee camp, dubbed Poverty Flat, complete with 110 tents, a commissary, and a latrine at each end of camp. The refugees ate army rations (mostly canned salmon) until supplies and food arrived from Mormon headquarters.

A month later they also abandoned Poverty Flat. When the government offered the refugees free railroad tickets to anywhere in the country, most of them joined relatives in Idaho, Utah, and California. One group founded a colony at Virden, above Lordsburg. Others filed homesteads on ranches in the Bootheel, while several families settled in Hachita.

The Mexican Revolution brought a certain prosperity to Hachita when the U.S. Army established Camp Shannon here in 1917 following Pancho Villa's raid on Columbus. The camp's 450 soldiers were assigned to protect the border from further incursions. Not only did the troops spend money in

Doomed to follow in the footsteps of its namesake, the village of Hachita has seen better days. Abandoned and decaying buildings share the dusty streets with mobile homes and well-maintained adobe houses.

town, but the army also bought supplies and services from Hachita businesses. For example, James Donaldson's butcher shop supplied the camp its beef, while Ole Peterson contracted to haul off its trash and Erastus Thygerson's carpenters helped build its fifty wood structures. In 1922, however, Camp Shannon closed and transferred its troops to Columbus. With them went Hachita's last brush with prosperity.

After World War I, falling copper prices caused the Arizona mines to cut production, which in turn reduced ore shipments on both railroad routes. The line from Morenci discontinued its leg to Hachita in 1934. When the border route from Douglas to El Paso shut down in 1961 and pulled up its tracks two years later, Hachita's railroad days were over. The high school closed in 1965 and the grade school two years later.

Today Hachita's old high school is an architectural oddity worthy of Ripley's record book. In the late 1970s a retired businessman from New York bought the school and spent five years transforming it into a Catholic church named in honor of his mother's patron saint. St. Catherine of Siena, with 100 tons of rock in its four-story facade, looms over the abandoned grade school next door.

A small adobe church nearby follows a more traditional line with tin-topped steeple and roof. It once was the Catholic church, and although a fence post sign identifies it as Your Church, nobody goes there at all. Still, the little church, like nearly all of Hachita's old buildings, seems the more lovely for its despair.

However, Hachita, population ninety-three, still has its post office.

▼ ▼ ▼ ▼ ▼ ▼ ▼ ▼ ▼ ▼ ▼   **Columbus**

Columbus is 31 miles south of Deming on NM 11 and 45 miles east of Hachita on NM 9.

Columbus is completely without pretense. Opinions receive a daily airing on the streets, while controversy takes its case to court or to the newspaper. Even the look of the town is unvarnished. Neighborhoods dress according to their own wishes, while churches bear names drawn out of a hat. The library's new digs are a former bar confiscated in a drug bust. It may not be pretty, but Columbus is very much alive!

Still, Columbus is not the town it used to be. In 1891, the Columbus town site was laid out three miles north of the Mexican border town of Palomas. Although promoters intended the new town to be a border station at the northern terminus of a Mexican railroad, that railroad never materialized. However, in 1903 the newly established El Paso and Southwestern Railroad made Columbus a stop on its way from Douglas, Arizona, to El Paso.

By 1905, Columbus was a solid railroad town with a population of 100, a general store, a saloon, and a customs inspector. Promoters attracted more settlers by touting the area's mineral-rich mountains and free, government-backed homesteads. Within a decade, Columbus had 700 people and a thriving business district that included a bank, four hotels, a jewelry store, and an ice cream parlor.

One of the early arrivals was Sam Ravel, a Jewish immigrant from El Paso, whose businesses in Columbus included a very successful general store and the two-story Commercial Hotel. James Dean, a retired lawyer from Iowa, was looking for opportunity and a little adventure when he took up homesteading nearby and opened a grocery store in town. Susan Parks came to Columbus with her husband, Garnet Parks, editor of the *Columbus Courier*. The weekly newspaper was published from their shop just west of the Hoover Hotel. The

A woman strikes a leisurely pose at the railroad station at Columbus sometime after 1909, when three trains a day stopped there. The last train stopped at Columbus on December 15, 1961. Courtesy Silver City Museum, #3277.

shop also was their home, from where Susan worked as the town's switchboard operator. On March 9, 1916, Sam Ravel and Garnet Parks both were out of town. On that day James Dean and Susan Parks would find their names forever linked with that of Pancho Villa.

Pancho Villa, the Mexican bandit and revolutionary, had suffered a bitter defeat by his rival Venustiano Carranza at Agua Prieta the previous November. Villa, who once had the backing of President Woodrow Wilson, was furious when Wilson threw his support behind Carranza. Wilson had allowed Carranza to ship 3,000 Mexican reinforcements by train across U.S. territory to Agua Prieta, thus ensuring Villa's defeat.

By now, Villa was desperate for guns and supplies. He was familiar with Columbus, previously having bought supplies from Sam Ravel's store. By one account Villa believed he still had credit at the store. By another account, Villa already had paid for the merchandise. Regardless, in February 1916, when Villa's general arrived at Ravel's to pick up guns and supplies, Ravel not only refused the order, he also threatened to throw the general out of the store. When Villa found out, he was enraged.

While the Mexican Revolution was boiling along the U.S. border, the residents at Columbus took comfort in the presence of Camp Furlong. The army camp, with its seven officers and 341 soldiers, was situated across from the train depot. However, in early March the post commander was warned that 500 Villistas were in the area. The *El Paso Times* reported on March 8 that Villa and his forces were camped fifteen miles west of Palomas. "What his plans are at this time is not known," the article said, but speculated that Villa might be planning an attack on Palomas.

Still, the residents of Columbus—as well as the army—were fast asleep when 500 Villistas stole across the border in the moonless early hours of March 9. Private Fred Griffin, who was on guard duty, was first to hear the horses. In the darkness, he challenged the riders and was shot dead by the first bullets of the raid. Suddenly mounted Villistas thundered through town,

To Mexican revolutionary Pancho Villa, the train depot was a landmark of the 1916 Columbus that he knew—a place he and his troops raided one spring night. He was pursued into Mexico by General John J. Pershing but not captured.

firing rifles and shouting, *"Viva Villa! Viva Mexico!"* One bullet slammed into the clock at the depot, stopping the hands at eleven minutes past four.

One group in search of Sam Ravel ransacked his store in the process. Other Villistas rushed the Commercial Hotel, shooting wildly. John W. Walker, who was in town for a Sunday school convention, was shot to death on the stairs in front of his bride of twenty-eight days. The Villistas dragged the others into the street, shot and killed three more men, then took aim at Walker's widow. When she blurted, *"Viva Mexico!"* the Villistas lowered their guns and let her go. Then they torched the hotel.

The shots that struck Private Griffin had alerted the troops at the camp. Lieutenant John P. Lucas, who commanded the machine gun group, dashed barefooted to a shack serving as a makeshift arsenal. He broke the door lock, then he and his men grabbed the machine guns. They set up near the depot to defend the south end of town. Lieutenant James P. Castleman led his troops through town, firing on the Mexicans by the light of the burning hotel. By then the entire business district was on fire. James Dean was shot and killed as he rushed down Main Street to help put out the fires.

Susan Parks woke with a start at the sound of gunfire. When she looked out the window, she recognized the horsemen in the street as Villistas. Quickly she gathered up her sleeping one-year-old daughter and ran across the room to the switchboard. But when she struck a match to see the telephone numbers, a spray of bullets shattered the window. Cut by the flying glass and bleeding, she crawled across the floor and stashed her crying baby beneath the bed. Then she went back to the switchboard and finally reached Captain A.W. Brock in Deming. For the next three hours, Susan Parks stayed at the switchboard while outside, troops battled the Villistas.

By 7:30 A.M. the raid was over and the Villistas had pulled back to Mexico with their spoils—300 rifles, eighty cavalry horses, and thirty mules. In the long chase to follow, however, the Mexicans lost most of their loot, including the horses. Back in Columbus, an entire block of the business district was burned to the ground. Soldiers collected ninety-three dead Villistas, piled them with the dead horses, then burned them all in one funeral pyre. The bodies of eighteen Americans killed in the attack were taken to the temporary morgue at the Columbus State Bank. Ten of the dead were civilians, including Bessie James, the pregnant wife of a railroad man.

Within a week, General John "Black Jack" Pershing and 5,000 troops were in pursuit of Villa into Mexico. During the next eleven months Columbus was headquarters for the Punitive Expedition, a force that eventually grew to 11,000 troops. While Villa was never caught (political enemies assassinated him in 1923), the expedition was a prelude to the U.S. entry into World War I. The expedition marked the end of the army's use of mounted cavalry and the beginning of its use of trucks and planes under combat conditions.

The U.S. Army used motorized trucks for the first time during the 1916 Punitive Expedition into Mexico. The army, however, still depended on mules to carry fuel for the trucks. Courtesy Museum of New Mexico, #5797. W. H. Horne Co. photograph.

In February 1917, Pershing's troops marched back into the United States. By May all the vehicles, airplanes, and machinery at Camp Furlong had been shipped out. In 1919, Columbus still served as field headquarters for 5,000 troops, but by 1923, the number had dwindled to sixty.

Columbus never rebuilt its gutted downtown. When the railroad shut down its route through Columbus in 1961, the town nearly died altogether. By 1970 the population was down to 241. But two decades later Columbus has revived as a border town of retirees, winter residents, and Mexican immigrants. Today some 1,700 people live in and around Columbus.

Those few buildings that survived the raid are nearly all in use. The U.S. Customs house is now the headquarters for Pancho Villa State Park. Plans to renovate the Hoover Hotel are on hold, but the building still stands. Classes are still held at the 1914 brick schoolhouse that served as a refuge during the raid. James Dean and Bessie James are buried in the Columbus cemetery at the western edge of town. The depot is now the Columbus Historical Museum, where according to the old clock high on the wall, it is always eleven minutes after four in the morning.

Pancho Villa State Park, (505) 531–2711, www.nmparks.com
Columbus Historical Museum, (505) 531–2620

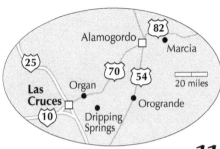

11 · The Southern Mountains:
Landscape of Lost Dreams

Organ · Dripping Springs · Orogrande · Marcia

These southern reaches were settled late by New Mexico standards. Don Juan de Oñate and his colonists hurried through the area in 1598 on their way north, where optimistic accounts of gold and civilization held greater promise. For more than two centuries southern New Mexico was left to the Apaches, who proved expert at wresting a living from these marginal lands. Then in the mid-1800s, with the Indian stronghold broken, men with big dreams began to tap the territory for its natural resources—gold, water, and timber, even its high mountain air. In the end nearly all the ventures either failed or ran a very short course. While most of the adventurers left to pursue other promises, many simply put down roots and stayed. Today Organ and Orogrande live as roadside towns with only one or two historical buildings left as evidence of an earlier life. Dripping Springs lies abandoned but protected in a narrow canyon, while the remnants of Marcia rest on a hillside under tall pines.

Organ

Organ is 17 miles east of Las Cruces on US 70. The old section of Organ is north of the highway.

Until the mid-1800s, Apaches held claim to the Organ Mountains. From these high hunting grounds they swept to the Jornada del Muerto below to raid passing caravans and to steal Spanish horses. Though the Apaches were little interested in mining themselves, their mountains would become central in New Mexico's mining history. Legend has it that in 1798 a dying

A rock house, situated at the base of the Organ Mountains between the mining town of Organ and the resort at Dripping Springs, is typical of the structures built during the turn-of-the-century mining boom.

One of the few recognizable historic buildings in Organ, the stone schoolhouse of the mining town faces an uncertain future, although it is encouraging to note the addition of a new tin roof, which will help protect the structure.

parishioner told a Jesuit priest of gold to be found in the Organ Mountains. Padre LaRue and his followers located the deposits and secretly mined the rich vein until the Catholic Church heard of his enterprise. To prevent authorities from taking the gold, the padre hid his cache in the mine and covered its entrance. When LaRue was murdered, the location of the mine was lost with him.

It is said that in 1849 a prospector searching for the Lost Padre Mine established the first mine in the Organ Mountains. He was soon bought out by Hugh Stephenson, who developed the mine as his own enterprise. In the ten years Stephenson worked the mine, optimistic reports claimed it produced $90,000 worth of silver and lead. By then as many as 149 miners lived in the Organ Mining District.

During the Civil War the Union Army confiscated the mine and the sixty-year-old Stephenson, a southern sympathizer, departed for Mexico.

The mining industry remained dormant throughout New Mexico during the war. However, when the war was over, many of the Union soldiers, who were California volunteers and veterans of the gold rush, opted to seek their fortunes in New Mexico's revived mining industry. At least a dozen California veterans staked claims in the Organs in the two decades after the war. One was Joseph F. Bennett, who bought into Stephenson's old mine, renaming it the Stephenson-Bennett Mine. By the 1880s, mines like the Modoc and the Torpedo were taking silver, lead, and copper from the Organ Mountains.

On February 26, 1885, the mining camp of Organ was patented as a township, boasting a population of 200. Organ had two general stores, seven saloons, a Catholic church, a schoolhouse—and a baseball team, the Organ Nine. *The Rio Grande Republican* reported that Organ defeated Las Cruces on July 4, 1884, in 108-degree heat. When the game was over, both sides celebrated with a "vigorous attack on the prize—a barrel of beer."

When Ben Jarratt moved his family to Organ in 1907, he quickly found work at one of the five lead mines operating twenty-four hours a day, all within walking distance of town. Jarratt rented a tent from Logan's Store as living quarters for his family of seven. Logan, who was nearly seven feet tall,

Taking a shady break in front of Bentley's Store in Organ are (left to right) Mr. Woodard, Mrs. Woodard, Mrs. Bentley, Mrs. Sweezey, Mr. Sweezey, and L. B. Bentley. The store was a central gathering place for Organ residents. Courtesy Rio Grande Historical Collections, New Mexico State University Library, Ms00140383. Louis B. Bentley Papers.

displayed his custom-made coffin in his store. He delighted in demonstrating its use by lying in it fully clothed, hands folded across his chest, eyes closed.

However, by the next year lead prices had hit bottom and Jarrett's young son was diagnosed with lead poisoning. The family moved on. Organ never regained its hold on history but for one last incident. On February 29, 1908, Pat Garrett rode from his ranch in the Organ Mountains, passing through town on his way to Las Cruces. On the road not far from Las Cruces, the old sheriff who had killed Billy the Kid was himself killed by a shot to the back of the head.

Nearly a century later, the only evidence of Organ's lively past is the schoolhouse, boarded up and minus its distinctive bell tower. Logan's Store is gone, but Bentley's Store and Assay Office, now a private residence, is still recognizable. Today Organ is occupied by small houses and worn-looking trailers. On the northeast edge of town Slumbering Mountain Cemetery overlooks the Jornada del Muerto far below. Fortune hunters still make occasional headlines as they search, always in vain, for the priest's lost mine. The only thing they'll find in Organ is his namesake street—Padre LaRue.

Dripping Springs

Dripping Springs is 10 miles east of Las Cruces on University Avenue, later Dripping Springs Road. The road is paved but for a 2.5-mile section. The hike to the resort is three miles round-trip over a rocky but fairly easy path with plenty of benches for shady stops.

More than twenty years ago, when we first hiked to Dripping Springs, we paid $1 at the ranch house for permission to take the rocky trail to the old mountain resort. Newly arrived in New Mexico and something of city slickers, we thought ourselves adventurous. When we reached the canyon, we were awed by our discovery. Steep canyon walls in shades of purple, olive, and rust harbored a stream filled with boulders torn from the mountain higher up. That spring day, however, the stream ambled lazily past leafy oak trees.

The old hotel, snug against the canyon wall, was a shell of rock and roof. We peeked in windows where wallpaper hung in strips, and we stood on its old porch, admiring the view of the valley below. Following a path past a stone water tank to a side canyon, we spotted a large wooden house and tiptoed inside for a better look. Practicing history by speculation, our children thought it might be a caretaker's house. We had the trail to ourselves on the way back and so, like latter-day von Trapps, we sang our way down the mountain.

When this wing was added to Van Patten's resort at the turn of the century, the Dripping Springs facility included thirty hotel rooms, a large dining room, a concert hall, and bandstand.

Today's trip is something of a pilgrimage, but with just two of us this time. We stop first to picnic at La Cueva, a sandstone formation whose peachy tones are warm and inviting on a winter afternoon. La Cueva, meaning "the cave," was home first to a prehistoric people who hunted in the grasslands below as far back as 7,000 years ago.

Sometime in the 1700s, roving bands of Apaches began taking shelter there. La Cueva's most famous occupant, however, was Agostini Justiniani, known as The Hermit, who arrived in the area in 1867. Agostini, son of Italian nobles, roamed three continents, ministering to natives wherever he went. He first showed up in New Mexico in Las Vegas, where he lived on a mountain known today as Hermit's Peak. When he took up residence at La Cueva, friends in Mesilla feared for his safety. He assured them he would make a fire every Friday in front of his cave to signal his well-being. But on April 17, 1868, there was no signal fire. His friends found him lying facedown

The walls of Van Patten's hotel are two feet thick and constructed of mud-plastered stone. The hotel originally had a covered porch. It is said that many famous people stayed here, including Pat Garrett and Pancho Villa.

with a knife in his back. His murder has never been solved. The restless hermit today is buried in Mesilla.

Just past La Cueva is the old ranch house, now the A.B. Cox Visitor Center, where hikers sign in before taking the trail to Dripping Springs. The health resort was originally known as Van Patten's Mountain Camp. New York-born Eugene Van Patten arrived in New Mexico in 1859, a twenty-year-old full of energy and ideas. In the late 1800s he had the idea of building a health resort on his Dripping Springs Canyon homestead some 6,000 feet high in the Organ Mountains. There patrons could find respite from the valley's summer heat. By 1906 the health resort included a thirty-two-room hotel, complete with shaded verandas, green lawns, and a bandstand. A stagecoach regularly made the seventeen-mile trip from Las Cruces to the hotel. Local Piro Indians who had helped build the hotel also staffed the resort and performed dances for the guests.

In 1917, however, Van Patten went bankrupt and sold Dripping Springs to Dr. Nathan Boyd. By that time, "altitude therapy" had become a popular method for treating tuberculosis, and Boyd's wife suffered from the lung disease.

Dr. Boyd also was a man of ideas. In 1895 the government had awarded

Colonel Eugene Van Patten is shown in his later years wearing his New Mexico National Guard uniform. Van Patten settled in Las Cruces in 1857 and was an important community leader for nearly seventy years. In addition to building Dripping Springs Resort, he was instrumental in bringing the railroad to Las Cruces and helped to secure a land grant for the Indians of Tortugas. Courtesy Rio Grande Historical Collections, New Mexico State University Library, RG84-7.

Boyd a construction permit to build a dam north of Las Cruces at a site called Elephant Butte. The permit gave him five years to complete the project. Legal battles with El Paso factions created enough delays, however, that Boyd lost the right to build the dam. Undaunted, he later helped establish a bank in Las Cruces and, of course, saw Van Patten's resort as choice property for his own sanatorium.

Boyd built his sanatorium near the reservoir Van Patten had built in 1892. Patients were housed in tents erected on stone foundations, the theory still holding that rest, good food, and exposure to fresh air cured tuberculosis. A wooden mess hall, the doctor's house, and later a caretaker's house completed the sanatorium. In 1922 Boyd sold out to Dr. Sexton, a Las Cruces physician, who continued to operate it as a sanatorium. By World War II new treatments, including drug therapy, eliminated the need for expensive altitude cures and Dripping Springs was abandoned.

This building served as the sanatorium's kitchen and dining room, where Dr. Boyd's tuberculosis patients took their meals.

Over the next half century vandals and weather tore at the buildings. Then in 1988 The Nature Conservancy bought the property, 2,800 acres, from the A. B. Cox family, then transferred the title to the Bureau of Land Management.

On today's hike we see that the old hotel has been stabilized, with remnants of the gold-striped wallpaper still hanging on for dear life. Boyd's mess hall and house remain, tidied and repaired. Nearby, stone foundations give clues to the tent quarters of patients who breathed the healing mountain air.

We no longer speculate on the history of Dripping Springs, as brochures and historical markers set the facts out for us. On the day we were there at least a dozen people milled around, keeping the sort of quiet usually reserved for museums. On our hike back down, we passed a dozen more headed up, including a couple pushing a jogging stroller where a baby was taking an afternoon nap.

A. B. Cox Visitor Center and Dripping Springs Recreation Area. Fee. (505) 525-4300.

Orogrande

Orogrande is 34 miles south of Alamogordo on US 54. The old school is about 100 yards off the highway at the north end of town. The road into the Jarilla Mountains is rough. Also, use caution when exploring the mining district.

Eugene Manlove Rhodes once got in a fight over a crap game in Orogrande. The western writer and cowboy, all 150 pounds of him, evened the odds against his huge opponent by bashing him with empty beer bottles. While they were patching the poor fellow up, Rhodes "absent-mindedly wandered off to New York." He didn't come back for twenty years.

Coincidental to Rhodes's leave-taking in the spring of 1906 was the arrival of a detachment of territorial mounted police who had come to town "to look after some beef-selling and a lot of hold-ups." Rhodes had been in Orogrande working on a pipeline project to bring water from the Sacramento Mountains fifty-five miles away to the mining camps in the Jarilla Mountains west of Orogrande. At the time, a minor gold rush had swelled Orogrande's population to 2,000 lively citizens.

The Jarilla Mountains, which rose to 4,800 feet above the dry, flat Tularosa Basin, were unremarkable in every aspect. Save one. The mountains were laced with turquoise, gold, silver, copper, and even coal. Established as a railroad stop in 1897, the place originally was called Jarilla Junction but was renamed "Big Gold," or Orogrande, when a six-and-a-half-ounce gold nugget

The desert mountains known as the Jarillas lured fortune seekers to the town of Orogrande—"Big Gold"—where this school was constructed during the boom days before the turn of the century.

was found in a dry wash. Mining investors happened to be looking on when the nugget was unearthed.

Developers quickly platted 5,000 town lots, offering them at $100 each. Soon Orogrande boasted a thirty-two-bed hospital, a hotel, and a weekly newspaper, plus the usual boomtown bars and brothels. Although gold never matched the promoters' promise, other minerals were found in such quantities that the railroad built spur lines into the Jarillas. There mining camps such as Brice grew large enough to support a school and its own saloon. By 1921, most of the mines had either played out or were no longer profitable. Miners, however, never gave up on the Jarillas.

Bill Ward landed in Orogrande thirty years ago after making stops at Arizona and Colorado mining towns. He does a little placer gold mining on his claim but says his take is "not enough to make a payday." He owns one of the two historical buildings in town, a dilapidated stone structure built around 1900 that once housed the general store, post office, and phone company. Ward and his nine-year-old granddaughter, Cassie, are partners in a mine tour business. She does the talking, he says, while he does the driving.

Cassie is at school today, so Ward does double duty. He follows a dirt road that forks and turns its way into the Jarillas, making his first stop at a current operation—an eighteen-foot hole in the ground dug by hand and neatly squared. Ward explains that many of the present-day claims are worked by "weekend miners." Farther into the hills Ward stops at what looks like, well, like nothing. As patiently as any archeologist, Ward points out shards of whiskey bottles, a rusty hinge, and stacks of rocks as evidence of the town of Brice. The mining camp once had 800 residents, a store, a saloon, and a

Cans are piled inside what once was the assay office for the Nanny Baird Mine. The old food cans were used as leaching agents in processing the ore. The area today can be "snaky" in summer.

Bill Ward and his granddaughter are collecting mining memorabilia, such as this old stove, in hopes of opening a mining museum in the "red barn" in Orogrande.

three-teacher school. The only thing left is the school's stone basement and a few scattered bricks from the teacherage.

"People who don't 'see' the real ghost town miss a lot," Ward says, picking up a rusted disk the size of a nickel. "This is a wallpaper tack from around 1900, so you know they at least had wallpaper then."

The Jarillas are pocked with abandoned mines. They range from surface, or placer, operations, to 400-foot shafts, to a strip mine that lays open a hillside's geologic history. In one cavern, oxidized copper streaks the ceiling in bright turquoise. But the mine is full of water and dangerous. Ward has a knowing respect for these open mines, which he says soon will be filled in or grated over to prevent accidents.

The old Brice Cemetery is a fitting last stop. A huge metal cross, painted bright white, is startling in this earthy setting. It was a gift of the Alamogordo Lions Club, an indestructible substitute for the bullet-riddled wooden cross nearby. Only a handful of tombstones remain, the names weathered to oblivion. Ward says one old tombstone had been lettered with inlaid turquoise but that the gems were later pecked out and the tombstone lost.

Marcia

The Marcia Cemetery is difficult to locate. However, if you want a picturesque ride up a pretty canyon, take NM 6563 from Cloudcroft for 10 miles toward Sunspot. Turn east on the Upper Rio Peñasco Road, which after about 3 miles becomes a dirt road. Go another mile to just past the second cattle guard. The cemetery is on the immediate left. It is on private property but can be seen from the road.

In 1898, Charles B. Eddy, who was adept at using other people's money, began building a railroad that would reach from El Paso north to the mines at White Oaks and on to join the Rock Island Line at Tucumcari. Eddy's entrepreneurial credits included founding the towns of Carlsbad (once named Eddy) and Alamogordo, plus involvement in a sundry of land, cattle, water, and mining ventures. The rail line paralleled the Sacramento Mountains, which Eddy planned to tap for their timber. He built a spur line into the mountains to retrieve cut spruce, pine, and oak. About a third of the timber would become railroad ties, with the rest to be used as mining timbers and as construction lumber.

Logging camps dotted the canyons along the spur line. Marcia, a camp

Serving the logging camps that popped up in the Sacramento Mountains, the Alamogordo and Sacramento Mountain Railway's remains are visible outside of Cloudcroft, where this impressive trestle spans Mexican Canyon.

in the Peñasco Canyon, became the logging headquarters, where equipment and engines were repaired and supplies were sold from the company store. It was a company town owned by the Southwest Lumber Company out of Alamogordo. With a turn-of-the-century population of about 100, Marcia supported a post office, the Marcia Mercantile, and a school that doubled as a dance hall on Saturdays and a church on Sundays. Marcia had its own country doctor, who tended to everything from treating injuries to pulling teeth to delivering babies.

In the early 1900s, young Edith Haught lived at Longwell Camp, some three miles from Marcia, with her widowed father and a brother and sister. In her memoir she wrote that Saturday in Marcia was "Dance and Fight Night." She said miners from Longwell would ride down to Marcia on a flatcar, pumping the handles to propel it along the tracks. On the way home, "the ones who could walk, pushed. Others not so sober rode in the car," she said. Entertainment also included boxing matches, poker games, and log-sawing contests. The self-described "logger's daughter" later married and raised a family on a farm not far from Marcia.

By the early 1940s the logging boom had long ceased and Marcia, along with other logging camps, was closing down. Finally in 1945, the railroad that created Marcia also closed. The last train out hooked up idle railroad cars and old engines for the trip down. Behind the train, workers pulled up the tracks for scrap metal. Marcia's buildings were scavenged for their wood. Today all that remains of Marcia is a hillside cemetery, where a few worn tombstones lie clustered inside a rusty iron fence.

The story of Marcia, however, is preserved in a 1905 log cabin saved from the camp and moved to the Pioneer Village and Historical Museum in Cloudcroft. The one-room cabin is furnished Logging Camp style. Also on the grounds is an 1887 cabin with lean-to additions that was home to Ed and Janie Posey and their twelve children. Members of the Posey family still live in the Cloudcroft area.

A logging family's "shack" is shown perched on a hillside in the Sacramento Mountains. The tent at the rear possibly served as the cook shack. Courtesy Rio Grande Historical Collections, New Mexico State University Library, Ms101. G. E. Miller photograph.

A few graves are scattered on the hillside cemetery at what was Marcia. Two new tombstones, both dated 1904, replace original grave markers, not uncommon in many of New Mexico's ghost town cemeteries.

The village also includes the summer cottage built by John Arthur Eddy, brother of Charles Eddy. While only two of the original eleven rooms have been saved, the 1899 cottage is the picture of Victorian ease.

And what of Charles Eddy? The old bachelor made a fortune from his New Mexico ventures only to lose most of it later in Mexican mining investments.

The Sacramento Mountains Historical Museum and Pioneer Village in Cloudcroft. Fee. (505) 682–2932.

Selected Readings

Anaya, Rudolfo A. *Bless Me, Ultima*. Berkeley, California: TQS Publications, 1972.

Austin, Mary. *The Land of Little Rain*. Albuquerque: University of New Mexico Press, 1974.

Barrington, Jacky, ed. *Celebrating 100 Years of Frontier Living*. Magdalena, N.Mex.: Magdalena Centennial Committee, 1984.

Beck, Warren A. *New Mexico: A History of Four Centuries*. Norman: University of Oklahoma Press, 1962.

Bolton, Herbert E. *Coronado: Knight of Pueblos and Plains*. Albuquerque: University of New Mexico Press, 1949.

Christiansen, Paige W. *The Story of Mining in New Mexico*. Socorro, N.Mex.: New Mexico Bureau of Mines & Mineral Resources, 1974.

Chronic, Halka. *Roadside Geology of New Mexico*. Missoula, Mont.: Mountain Press Publishing Co., 1987.

Clark, Ira G. *Water in New Mexico: A History of Its Management and Use*. Albuquerque: University of New Mexico Press, 1987.

Davis, W.W. H. *El Gringo: New Mexico and Her People*. Lincoln: University of Nebraska Press, 1982.

Dean, Richard. "The Columbus Story." Columbus, N.Mex.: 1994.

Emmett, Chris. *Fort Union and the Winning of the Southwest*. Norman: University of Oklahoma Press, 1965.

Fugate, Francis L., and Roberta B. Fugate. *Roadside History of New Mexico*. Missoula, Mont.: Mountain Press Publishing Co., 1989.

García, Nasario. *Recuerdos de los Viejitos: Tales of the Rio Puerco*. Albuquerque: Historical Society of New Mexico and University of New Mexico Press, 1987.

———. *Más Antes: Hispanic Folklore of the Rio Puerco Valley*. Santa Fe: Museum of New Mexico Press, 1997.

Gregg, Josiah. *Commerce of the Prairies*. Norman: University of Oklahoma Press, 1954.

Hall, Linda B., and Don M. Coerver. *Revolution on the Border: The United States and Mexico, 1910–1920*. Albuquerque: University of New Mexico Press, 1988.

Harris, Linda G. *Las Cruces: An Illustrated History*. Las Cruces, N.Mex.: Arroyo Press, 1993.

Hill, Rita. "Then and Now, Here and Around Shakespeare." Lordsburg, N.Mex.: Lordsburg, Hidalgo County Chamber of Commerce, 1963.

Hilliard, George. *Adios Hachita: Stories of a New Mexico Town*. Silver City, N.Mex.: High-Lonesome Books, 1998.

———. *A Hundred Years of Horse Tracks: The Story of the Gray Ranch*. Silver City, N.Mex.: High-Lonesome Books, 1996.

Hoover, H.A. *Tales from the Bloated Goat: Early Days in Mogollon*. El Paso: Texas Western Press, 1958.

Horgan, Paul. *Lamy of Santa Fe*. New York: Farrar, Strauss and Giroux, 1975.

Huber, Joe. *The Story of Madrid, New Mexico*. n.p., n.d.

Hutchinson. W.H. *A Bar Cross Man: The Life and Personal Writings of Eugene Manlove Rhodes*. Norman: University of Oklahoma Press, 1956.

Jensen, Joan M., and Darlis A. Miller. *New Mexico Women: Intercultural Perspectives*. Albuquerque: University of New Mexico Press, 1986.

Julyan, Robert. *The Place Names of New Mexico*. Albuquerque: University of New Mexico Press, 1998.

Lane, Lydia Spencer. *I Married a Soldier*. Albuquerque: University of New Mexico Press, 1987.

Larson, Carole. *Forgotten Frontier: The Story of Southeastern New Mexico*. Albuquerque: University of New Mexico Press, 1993.

Lawson, Jacqueline E. *Cerrillos: Yesterday, Today and Tomorrow*. Santa Fe: Sunstone Press, 1989.

Looney, Ralph. *Haunted Highways: The Ghost Towns of New Mexico*. New York: Hastings House Publishers, 1968.

Lorence, James J. *The Suppression of Salt of the Earth: How Hollywood, Big Labor, and Politicians Blacklisted a Movie in Cold War America*. Albuquerque: University of New Mexico Press, 1999.

Lynn, Sandra D. *Windows on the Past: Historic Lodging of New Mexico*. Albuquerque: University of New Mexico Press, 1999.

Mangan, Frank. *Ruidoso Country*. El Paso: Mangan Books, 1994.

McKenna, James A. *Black Range Tales: Chronicling Sixty Years of Life and Adventure in the Southwest*. Glorieta, N.Mex.: The Rio Grande Press, Inc., 1936.

Meltzer, Richard. *Madrid Revisited: Life and Labor in a New Mexican Mining Camp in the Years of the Great Depression*. Santa Fe: The Lightning Tree, 1976.

Metz, Leon C. *Pat Garrett: The Story of a Western Lawman*. Norman: University of Oklahoma Press, 1974.

Miller, Darlis A. *Soldiers and Settlers: Military Supply in the Southwest 1861–1885*. Albuquerque: University of New Mexico Press, 1989.

Murphy, Larry. *Out in God's Country: A History of Colfax County, New Mexico*. Springer, N.Mex.: Springer Publishing Co., 1969.

Myers, Lee. "Fort Stanton, New Mexico: The Military Years, 1855–1896." Lincoln, N.Mex.: Lincoln County Historical Society Publications, July 1988.

Myrick, David F. *New Mexico's Railroads: A Historical Survey*. Albuquerque: University of New Mexico Press, 1990.

Neal, Dorothy Jensen. *The Cloud Climbing Railroad*. Alamogordo, N.Mex.: Alamogordo Printing Co., 1966.

Pearson, Jim Berry. *The Maxwell Land Grant*. Norman: University of Oklahoma Press, 1961.

Rakocy, Bill. *Ghosts of Kingston, Hillsboro, N. Mex*. El Paso: Bravo Press, 1983.

Roberts, Susan A., and Calvin A. Roberts. *New Mexico*. Albuquerque: University of New Mexico Press, 1988.

Riskin, Marci L. *New Mexico's Historic Places: The Guide to National and State Register Sites*. Santa Fe: Ocean Tree Books, 2000.

Sherman, James, and Barbara H. Sherman. *Ghost Towns and Mining Camps of New Mexico*. Norman: University of Oklahoma Press, 1975.

Simmons, Marc. *The Last Conquistador: Juan de Oñate and the Settling of the Far Southwest*. Norman: University of Oklahoma Press, 1991.

———. *New Mexico: An Interpretive History*. Albuquerque: University of New Mexico Press, 1977.

———. *Turquoise and Six-Guns*. Santa Fe: Sunstone Press, 1974.

Smith, Toby. *Coal Town: The Life and Times of Dawson, New Mexico*. Santa Fe: Ancient City Press, 1993.

Sonnichsen, C.L. *Tularosa: Last of the Frontier West*. Albuquerque: University of New Mexico Press, 1980.

———. *The Mescalero Apaches*. Norman: University of Oklahoma Press, 1958.

Stanley, F. "The Colfax, New Mexico Story." Pep, Tex.: n.p., January 1967.

———. "The Johnson Mesa, New Mexico Story." Pep, Tex.: n.p., May 1965.

———. "The Dawson Tragedies." Pep, Tex.: n.p., December 1964.

———. "The Hillsboro, New Mexico Story." Pep, Tex.: n.p., August 1964.

———. "The Sugarite, New Mexico Story." Pep, Tex.: n.p., June 1964.

———. "The Yankee, New Mexico Story." Pep, Tex., n.p., July 1964.

———. "The Georgetown, New Mexico Story." Pep, Tex.: n.p., May 1963.

———. "The Folsom, New Mexico Story." Pantex, Tex.: n.p., February 1962.

———. "The Watrous, New Mexico Story." Pantex, Tex.: n.p., August 1962.

———. "The Dawson, New Mexico Story." Pantex, Tex.: n.p., September 1961.

———. "The Kingston, New Mexico Story." Pantex, Tex.: n.p., August 1961.

Townsend, David, and Clif McDonald. *Centennial: Where the Old West Meets the New Frontier*. Alamogordo, N.Mex.: Alamogordo/Otero Centennial Celebration, Inc., 1999.

Townsend, Lennie, ed. *Things Remembered: Otero County, New Mexico, 1899–1999*. Alamogordo, N.Mex.: Alamogordo/Otero Centennial Celebration, Inc., 1998.

Trigg, Maggie Day. *Cerrillos Adventure at the Bar T H Ranch*. Santa Fe: Sunstone Press, 1985.

Tweit, Susan. *The Great Southwest Nature Factbook*. Seattle: Alaska Northwest Books, 1992.

Utley, Robert M. *Fort Union and the Santa Fe Trail*. Southwest Studies Series No. 89. Texas Western Press, University of Texas at El Paso, 1989.

———. *High Noon in Lincoln: Violence on the Western Frontier*. Albuquerque: University of New Mexico Press, 1987.

Varney, Philip. *New Mexico's Best Ghost Towns*. Albuquerque: University of New Mexico Press, 1987.

Watson, Dorothy. "The Pinos Altos Story." n.p.: n.p., 1960.

Williams, Jerry L., ed. *New Mexico in Maps*. Albuquerque: University of New Mexico Press, 1986.

Wilson, Delphine Dawson. *John Barkley Dawson: Pioneer, Cattleman, Rancher*. n.p.: n.p., 1997.

Wilson, John P. *Merchants, Guns, and Money: The Story of Lincoln County and Its Wars*. Santa Fe: Museum of New Mexico Press, 1987.

Index